W9-ANN-580

The
in T

The Upper Limb in Tetraplegia

A New Approach to Surgical Rehabilitation

By Erik Moberg

30 Figures in 65 Individual Presentations
9 Tables

Georg Thieme Publishers Stuttgart 1978

Erik A. Moberg, M. D., Professor emeritus of Orthopedic and Hand Surgery.
Former Chief, Department I of Orthopedic and Hand Surgery, Sahlgren's Hospital,
University of Göteborg, Sweden.
Förtroligheten 50, 412 70, Göteborg, Sweden

CIP-Kurztitelaufnahme der Deutschen Bibliothek

Moberg, Erik:
The upper limb in tetraplegia : a new
approach to surg. rehabilitation. – Stuttgart :
Thieme, 1978.
   ISBN 3-13-508101-X

© 1978 Georg Thieme Verlag, Herdweg 63, P.O.B. 732, D-7000 Stuttgart 1
Printed in Germany, typeset by Bauer & Bökeler KG, Denkendorf, on Linofilm Europa
»S«; printed by Illig, Göppingen
ISBN 3-13-508101-X

Preface

The facts presented in this volume have emerged by an amalgamation of unusual circumstances. The work started at the Department of Orthopedic and Hand Surgery at the Sahlgren's Hospital, University of Göteborg. It was based on decades of experience in reconstructive surgery with subsequent rehabilitation and with associated research work. What made the whole possible was the cooperation from, first of all, hundreds of patients, many of them not even able to understand my attempts at different languages, and from colleagues and institutions in many countries. By intensive travelling the work could be continued in other parts of Sweden and Scandinavia.

Of paramount importance was the efforts of Vernon L. Nickel, MD, former chief, Surgical Services and Spinal Cord Injury Department at the world-famous Rancho Los Amigos Hospital in Downey, California. Together with Juan E. Fonseca, MD, former chief of Spinal Cord Injury Service at the Veterans Administration Hospital, Long Beach, California, he was the leading stimulus in the arrangement of my periods as Visiting Professor at the University of California, Irvine, involving clinical work for the two services mentioned. Together they include more beds for spinal injuries than can be found at any other single place.

Of the many other colleagues who have placed their knowledge and experience at my disposal, I have mentioned some in the text, but should like to record here my special indebtedness to Professor Olle Höök, MD, Head of Rehabilitation Services, Associate Professor Svante Edshage, MD, my successor as Head of the Department of Hand Surgery, and Ann Mari Broman, MD, all of Sahlgren's Hospital, University of Göteborg, Sweden; Knud Bang-Rasmussen, MD, former Head of the Department of Hand Surgery, Ortopedisk Hospital, Copenhagen, Denmark; and Professor Lars Erik Laurent, MD, Director, Invalidstiftelsen, Helsingfors, Finland.

Arnold Graham Smith, MD, FRCS, with whom I worked at the Rancho Los Amigos Hospital, has taken great paints to put my manuscript into readable English. The majority of the photos originate from Sahlgren's Hospital and the Veterans Administration Hospital; additional illustrations and material were provided by the other hospitals mentioned and by the Journal of Bone and Joint Surgery and the Journal of Hand Surgery, to whom I am indebted for permission to reproduce. The work has been supported by grants from the Greta and Einar Askers Stiftelse, Göteborg, and publication made possible by a generous guarantee from Medicinska Forskningsradet, Stockholm.

The basis here described for evaluation and treatment can be said to rest on firm scientific ground, but development goes on, not without speed. By the time the book goes into print, there may already, be new technical improvements for elbow extension (which may raise the percentage of patients who can be given some help above the 70 % now in reach); the Zancolli "lasso" operation may have got wider application; more will be known about proprioception and also about contractures. And so the whole field, rather than being stationary, is in cautious movement ahead. The Small Group International Conference recently held in Edinburg supported this view.

The new approach will be of use also in the treatment of major functional loss caused by other diseases.

Göteborg, June 1978   Erik Moberg

Contents

Introduction

During the last few decades, astonishing developments in the treatment of tetraplegic patients have occurred, many of which were initiated by the work of Sir Ludwig Guttmann. Improved prophylactic care has greatly reduced acute systemic sequelae, urinary infections, and pressure sores which, up to now, led to shortened life expectancy. All these advances have in common the fact that they have diminished complications.

But in spite of all these efforts, progress in making *positive* contributions to improve the patient's new way of life has been restricted to such endeavors as increasing mobility with more efficient wheelchairs and automobiles, providing proper social security benefits, providing adequate living accommodation, and promoting participation in special sporting events. The possibility of improving the function of the hands and arms would be an important additional contribution, as there is much truth in the saying that "their hands are their life".

Both active and passive splinting in their various forms have been helpful in many cases, but reconstructive upper limb surgery, especially hand surgery, has as yet made only a small contribution. The number of cases operated on with good results is very small and most centers have had little or no experience at all in this field. It cannot be denied that some of the earlier efforts, despite the best of intentions, have even resulted in functional loss.

Thanks to a background of long experience in general surgery, orthopedic surgery and hand surgery, I was able to start work in this field as soon as I was freed from the heavy administrative and routine clinical work involved in running a large university hospital department. This had been my ambition for a long time.

Because of the totally different physiological basis from which the hand of the tetraplegic must function, it is my opinion that the routine methods of evaluating the functions of the hand will not suffice here and that a new basic approach must be worked out. The work could proceed only in steps, and the new conception, of course, must be based on the basic rule of "non nocere".

The actual realization of this approach was started and developed in Scandinavia but good fortune has allowed me to continue the work in large centers located in other countries. In particular, I would like to mention the large Spinal Cord Injury Centers at the Veterans Administration Hospital, Long Beach, and at the Rancho Los Amigos Hospital in Downey, both in California.

Collaborators in various positions and patients have contributed, and continue to do so, their new points of view and helped me obtain a better understanding of the quite special conditions to be observed here. However, it seems that the time has come to bring together all the unique experience gained, as already described, in spite of the fact that work in this field has only just started. The first results are so incomplete that some of the yet unresolved problems are listed in a special chapter. There is still much research to be done.

The problem is not a small one. In Sweden, my own small country, we are dealing with approximately sixty new tetraplegic cases a year, and as the estimated life expectancy is several decades the total and steadily increasing number is important. Some 50000 paralyzed patients are believed to exist in the United States today and two thirds of them are cases of tetraplegia, the majority being victims of traffic accidents. Research work in England and other countries shows that the number of tetraplegic cases is going up as compared to the paraplegic ones. Most of them need help every day. It is usually the young and daring men who suffer this enormous handicap.

A recent survey (Hanson and Franklin 1976) shows beyond doubt that the function tetraplegics most badly want to regain is the use of their arms and hands. A number of these patients at two Veterans Administration Hospitals were shown four cards entitled: (1) normal use of your legs, (2) normal use of your bowel and bladder functions, (3) normal feeling and use of your sexual organs, (4) normal use of your arms and hands. The patients were asked to list these four items in order of importance. Of these patients 75,7 % gave as first choice the return of the function of their arms and hands, 13.5 % chose alternative (2), 8.1 % chose alternative (1) and only 2.7 % found alternative (3) to be most important. It should also be remembered that rehabilitation to a degree that will make employment possible almost always requires the function of arms and hands with greater efficiency than can be obtained without surgery. A new approach to the problem is important.

Earlier Approaches to the Field. Comments

The earliest attempt to improve the gripping function of the hands in tetraplegia seems to have been made in Germany in 1920 (Schmidt and Schrauder). Really good flexor hinge splints were constructed, but due to the very short life expectancy and the poor physical shape of the patients at that time, they were not widely used. The existence of such devices was forgotten. Subsequently, through the work already mentioned, the condition of the patients had improved very much. And now the time had come to rediscover the means to improve the gripping functions. This occurred independent of the earlier work. In a paper published by Rancho Los Amigos Hospital in 1963 by Nickel et al, active splinting was recommended and details were given. There is no doubt that these splints gave many patients opportunities for independent activities such as dressing and feeding themselves, writing, and also getting some kind of employment. In different countries extensive work continues on the development of splinting and electronic devices which are especially helpful to patients with a higher level of tetraplegia which leaves no scope for modern surgical methods. However, the disadvantages are obvious as with all kinds of splinting, orthoses and prostheses. Their role in permanent use for the tetraplegic patient is beyond the scope of this book.

Sterling Bunnell was probably the first to approach by surgery the restoration of some gripping functions of the hand in tetraplegia. A short discussion of principles appeared in the second edition of *Surgery of the Hand* (1948). Bunnell suggested flexor tenodeses and also similar procedures for thumb opposition. Only the surgical procedures are discussed, no cases or results are mentioned. Similar procedures were realized by Street and Stambaugh (1959) and by Wilson (1956). But it was still too early for surgery in spite of reported useful results in a very limited number of cases.

Thus tetraplegia seems to have been a neglected, indeed almost a forbidden field for modern hand surgery, with the few exceptions mentioned below. Very few centers for tetraplegia have any experience at all and strong voices have even spoken against surgery in this field, no doubt because of a few unsuccessfull cases. It is of interest to note that the book by Michaelis (1964) on surgery in paraplegia deals mainly with the lower extremity. One exception, however, is the case where wrist extension and the limited hand function present was lost when attempting to use the extensor carpi radialis longus as a transfer. It was expected that the brevis would be strong enough for wrist extension, but it was not. Michaelis restored the original situation by surgery. I have also seen a few similar cases operated on elsewhere and have had to reconstruct one of them (p. 82).

Other reports were made concerning attempts to achieve a pinch by stabilization by fusion of several finger joints combined with muscle transfers. This work was based partly on the experience in the treatment of polio hands (Nickel et al. 1963, Buck-Gramcko 1967), but the results did not lead to the continued use of these methods. Obviously the pinch obtained did not compensate for the loss of other functions, and the number of cases was small. Difficulties occurred in handling wheelchairs, in transfer and with human contact which requires soft flexible hands. Thus, it was necessary to explore other ways to improve function by surgery.

A number of later contributions dealt mainly with the small group of tetraplegic patients who have several muscles available for wrist and hand motion and, there-fore, also for surgical transfer. The very inaccurate classification based on the so-called "neurological level" puts them in the C6 to C8 groups, frequently classified as "incomplete". But, as will be seen below, some of these earlier papers start with an explanation that this classification leaves the surgeons without help when discussing indications and results. Different new ways to classify are suggested, but these are still not as clear as could be desired. This means that from the information given in these publications it is rarely possible to analyze the loss and what is left with certainty. It is thus impossible to compare the results from different ap-proaches.

Sensibility is only occasionally mentioned, but no details are given. The muscle power of the different muscles in separate cases is usually impossible to evaluate. Only a few reports describe results in a way which makes it possible to grade them for comparison. About the only area left open for discussion is that of different surgical approaches.

Lipscomb et al (1958) made a very serious early attempt to approach the problems of reconstruction. They report 11 cases with 21 hands operated on. This is one of the few works in which, in the great majority of patients, both sides were operated on. The descriptions of what functions remained are so accurate that it is possible to assess the cases by my own classification (Chapter 4). There are ten OCu:3 hands; four OCu:2; three OCu:4; two OCu:6; and two belonging to the group OCu:1. The hand not operated on was an OCu:8 hand.

In the majority of cases, flexor carpi radialis was used for what is called "thumb opposition". In some cases flexor carpi ulnaris was used. The pronator teres in most cases was used for finger flexion and brachioradialis for thumb flexion. The Rior-dan intrinsic tenodesis was used in seven hands to prevent metacarpophalangeal hyperextension. Finger extension was usually achieved by transfer of extensor carpi radialis longus, or, if this was not possible, by extensor tenodesis.

It is interesting to see, that in the two hands where only the wrist extensors were strong enough for use (OCu:1) and where tenodeses were the only possible proce-dures, functional gain was as good as or better than some cases with many more muscles available. Fifty-six operations were performed on 21 hands ranging from ten to two (the OCu:1 case) for each pair of hands. The authors, however, state that they believe two operations on each hand could be sufficient when more experience was gained. The pictures show that side pinch was obtained, not real opposition.

A continuation of this work was presented as a paper given at the meeting of the American Society for Surgery of the Hand in January 1970 but published only as a short review (Henderson et al. 1970). The full manuscript, however, has been made available to me by kind permission of the authors. It evaluates the effect of these surgical procedures in 41 patients and compares their overall function with that of 19 patients who had similar lesions but were not operated on. Of the 41 patients operated on 32 could be followed up for more than two years, eighteen of them were gainfully employed, compared with only three of 11 patients followed up from the 19 who had no surgery. The authors conclude that a comparison of the hand function "indicated that the percentage of patients, who had significant improvement, was higher among those who were operated on than among those who were not. Although many complications and disappointments are associated with these procedures, and although the length of hospitalization is significant, the end results seem to justify continuing this approach to the problem of the tetraplegic".

Lamb has reported reconstructive work in four papers (1963, 1971, 1972 and 1976), some of which were written together with Landry. Out of a group of 113 patients examined 25 received operative treatment. It was not possible to find out in how many cases both hands were operated on.

The authors stress the fact that it is of no use to classify the patients according to "anatomical levels of cord damage". They say that what matters is which muscles are still active. Most patients fit into a characteristic group, even if there are exceptions. The levels for which surgery has nothing to offer are classified as groups 1 and 2. Their group 3 cases have pronation, supination and wrist extensors strong enough to let the extensor carpi radialis brevis perform wrist extension by itself. The basis for their reconstruction is also wrist extension. Sensibility is described as "satisfactory in the hands" but no details are given. In this group, three out of thirteen patients were operated on. Extensor carpi radialis longus was used as a transfer to flexor digitorum profundus, and brachioradialis was transferred to flexor pollicis longus. Attempts were made to get thumb opposition by tenodesis, but these seemed to have been less successful. The authors' experience evidently made them prefer a "side pinch". Of the thirteen cases, eleven were improved, two unimproved, and no one lost function.

The cases in group 4 also have the flexor carpi radialis functioning. When elbow extension is present, described as a great functional benefit, the cases are brought into a special group 5, and when the finger extensors are also spared, they form group 6. For the groups 4 to 6, however, the basis of the surgical procedure was unchanged. This was the same as for group 3 with the addition of the construction of an opposition pinch with transfer of the flexor carpi radialis, elongated by a free tendon graft or a ring finger sublimis tendon.

Lamb has also tried the Lipscomb procedure with one active extensor and one active flexor; however, he found his own way better, relying on potentiated natural tenodesis to produce finger flexion when the wrist extends. In this group, six cases were operated on and five were improved.

Group 7 had only the loss of intrinsic function and a "standard Bunnell adduction-opponensplasty (1948)" was performed. Both hands were operated on at the patients request and all improved. The authors found the extensor pollicis brevis tendon unsatisfactory for the opponensplasty. They did not find wrist arthrodesis useful. Spasticity was always taken as a contraindication to reconstructive surgery. I recently (November 1976) visited Lamb and saw quite a few of his cases. The number of cases operated on had increased and the finger gripping function was good and useful. Only in one case was finger flexion exaggerated and the extension of the fingers was insufficient. He had also started to perform the deltoid transfer (Moberg) for elbow extension.

In two papers Freehafer has made a valuable contribution to this surgery. In the first paper (Freehafer and Mast 1967) seven cases were reported in which a successful transfer of the brachioradialis tendon was performed to increase very weak wrist extension, the basis of hand functioning in tetraplegia. However, the strength was not enough to make use of active splinting.

The second paper (Freehafer et al. 1974) describes operations on 24 hands in 20 patients selected from more than 350 patients examined. Good results were often achieved using tendon transfers to provide finger flexion and what is called "opposition". Their surgery differs from several other accounts in that they were usually working on only one hand.

Freehafer and coworkers also state that they found little value in a classification of the patients based on the so-called neurological level when evaluating hands for surgery and discussing results. They suggest their own classification based on the function that is left. They also stress the importance of sensory evaluation, but do not bring this into the classification. This differs from that of Lamb in minor details and in the numbers applied to the groups, but it is basically constructed in the same way. However, a special group 6 is added for the cases which do not fit into the other five groups.

They also mentioned that occasionally spasticity, when present in a moderate degree, instead of being a contraindication to surgery might even be helpful in increasing the power to grip.

Two kinds of transfers were used: A. transfer for "opposition", B. transfer for finger flexion.

A. As donor muscles for "opposition", flexor carpi radialis, brachioradialis and extensor carpi radialis were used in that order of preference. As donor tendon, they used superficialis to the ring finger in situ with distal detachment and insertion into the abductor brevis tendon of the thumb. In a few cases the rerouted extensor pollicis brevis crossing the palm was used, but, like Lamb, they found this was not as good.

B. To restore voluntary finger flexion, flexor carpi radialis, pronator teres, brachioradialis, or extensor carpi radialis longus muscle was used. It is stressed that the use of the latter is not safe as the brevis may not be strong enough for good wrist extension. Useful results were obtained in all cases except for one which later had an ascending paralysis. No true opposition was obtained, but rather a side pinch. When brachioradialis was used as motor, the pinch power was not more than 0.2 kg in several cases. After the finger flexion transfer some of the hands tended to go into more flexion than desired with some loss of extension. The authors, therefore, questioned whether the procedure should not be limited to just one hand. Arthrodeses of multiple joints should be avoided and they also found no indication for wrist fusion. Transfer for thumb flexion was not considered useful.

Zancolli has great experience in this field, documented in a series of published and unpublished papers (1968, 1969, 1975). He has very kindly given me parts of the unpublished manuscripts and pictures to study, they show an interesting development in technique and methods not yet used by other surgeons. Like Freehafer,

Lamb and myself, he has found classification according to the neurological level too inexact for grouping his cases and unsatisfactory as a basis for surgical evaluation. He describes four main groups, each divided up into two subgroups. His experience is based on 97 patients of whom 76 had surgical procedures. Only patients considered for surgery were included. It is not possible to find out in how many or in which cases reconstructions were performed on both sides.

Group 2 was the largest and contained 74 % of his cases. These were the patients with wrist extension and all could be helped in some way. In 82 % of the 74 this movement was strong, but in the remaining 18 % it was weak. The weak group got weak lateral pinch and grip and the others got the same grip in function, but this was better if the muscles were stronger or if flexor carpi radialis, pronator teres, and/or triceps were also present. The side pinch and not opposition was the aim for the thumb action. The surgery, as in Lipscomb's cases, is always divided into two steps. The first is the extensor phase, including fusion of the thumb carpometacarpal joint, and occasional stabilization of the metacarpophalangeal (MCP) joint with a capsuloplasty. It also includes the transfer of brachioradialis to the long extensor tendons of the fingers and the thumb as well as stabilization of the MCP joints of the fingers, if necessary by transferring the paralyzed superficialis. If pronator teres is present, sometimes it is used for wrist flexion if this function is absent.

The second step, the flexor phase, four to six months later, includes the transfer of extensor carpi radialis longus to flexor profundus and the activation of flexor pollicis longus. In some cases a tenodesis was performed. An interesting detail is that sometimes the flexor pollicis longus tendon could be joined sideways to the extensor carpi radialis brevis to obtain an active function as it appears not to disturb the function of the latter muscle. Rarely, a supernumerary wrist extensor muscle or more often fibrous bands are used for some additional function or for thumb flexion. On the whole Zancolli has attempted more elaborate and complicated reconstructions than the other authors reviewed here. He has tried dermatodeses and capsulodeses, but obviously found them not sufficiently resistant to time and wear. Without giving detailed case reports, he concludes that the function the patient can be given is better than can be provided by splinting. Therefore, in the absence of surgical contraindications, the patient should be operated. In groups 3 and 4 (6.8 % and 6.2 %) more transfers could, of course, be used and more function obtained. No surgery was performed earlier than five months following the accident and most cases were operated on before eighteen months had passed.

In April 1977, I had the opportunity of visiting Dr. Zancolli in Buenos Aires. In a most helpful way he showed me his cases, demonstrated surgery and we did several cases together. We discussed the whole subject of surgery in tetraplegia. Obviously, however, our cases were different. A comparison was made and the result is given in Chapter 6.

Dr. Zancolli also confirmed that he had given up fasciodermatodesis, capsulorrhaphy and some more complicated variations which did not prove strong enough for prolonged active use. Only at the thumb's metacarpophalangeal joint does he use capsulorrhaphy, reinforced by bony fixation of a sesamoid bone. He had the same difficulty as the author, in getting the brachioradialis to function satisfactorily after a transfer in the absence of an antagonistic function of the triceps. A case was demonstrated in which this muscle had been transferred to the finger extensors. However, the fingers could only be extended actively when elbow flexion was prevented by bracing the dorsal surface of the hand against the chin.

His new "lasso" operation for clawing is described in Chapter 8.

The valuable experience of McDowell, hitherto only very briefly published 1971, has been made available through the kindness of the author himself. He gave me a small "workbook" to evaluate with six pages of text and some interesting tables. He had examined over 100 cases and also operated on many of them, although the exact number is unknown.

He, too, has found difficulties with the so-called "neurological" classification; he therefore describes his own, based on the muscles left. Five groups are discussed, differing little from those of Lipscomb and Freehafer. McDowell stresses the importance of constructing the grip on the basis of the natural tenodesis effect. Psychoneurosis and severe spasticity are contraindications and the least complex surgery is the best. He uses mechanical appliances even in cases where strong wrist dorsiflexion was made possible only by tendon transfer. In his group 4, which seems to correspond to my group OCu-3, the surgery is similar to that of Lipscomb and coworkers. Group 5 seems to have residual functions similar to my OCu-6 cases, and the very best group (group 6) lacks only the intrinsics. For the last three groups, an opponens transfer is performed using brachioradialis, flexor carpi radialis, or flexor carpi ulnaris, Phalangeal fusions are included in the treatment for group 5; for the flexors a tenodesis of profundus is used. Intrinsic replacement is recommended for group 6, but no details are given. In another very short abstract of a paper given to the International Society for Quadriplegia in 1972, the same author describes six cases in which brachioradialis was used for wrist extension in patients with inadequate extensors. The technique was the same as that used by Freehafer. Five of the patients could later dorsiflex against five pounds and could grip by using braces. The author found the radial deviation of the wrist cumbersome and he tested "bridle" arrangements to avoid this. My own comment on this is that in the surgical technique (p. 47) to get the thumb action in a key grip by means of the flexor pollicis longus tenodesis described below, the radial deviation is useful as it makes it easier for the hand to meet the thumb in a good grip. This is preferable to using a brace.

Finally, McDowell has tried to use the biceps as a wrist extensor, joining it to the extensor carpi radialis brevis with free tendon grafts. Some wrist extension was achieved in two cases, but he considers this transfer "not indicated instead of a brace with external power source until the technique can be refined" (see also p. 50 on the value of an antagonist muscle).

In 1976 House et al. published a paper dealing with reconstructive work on seven patients with tetraplegia. The condition of six patients was improved. In three of them both hands were operated on, making a total of ten hands; all belonging to what is called "strong C6 and C7" levels. House and coworkers give functional priority to restoration of active digital flexion. For finger flexion they prefer a transfer of extensor carpi radialis longus to flexor digitorum profundus. They talk about an adduction-opponensplasty, but it is obvious that what they really want to achieve is a side pinch – a key grip. The superficialis tendon from the ring finger, partially in situ, is used to transfer the motor power from the pronator teres, brachioradialis, flexor carpi radialis or ulnaris to the new insertion on the thumb. This is performed into the adductor pollicis and the extensor pollicis longus tendons. If there are remaining muscles available to use for a transfer, a flexor pollicis longus is added or reinforced. The surgery is divided into an extensor phase, sometimes including intrinsic tenodesis of the index and middle fingers, and a flexor phase. The average grasp and pinch force postoperatively was 5.5 kg and 3.0 kg respectively. The follow-up time for four cases was six years, five and one-half years, four years, and two years respectively, but for the rest it was much shorter.

My paper published in 1975 gives a totally new approach to the classification based on the afferent impulses present for controlling the grip. Each arm is classified separately. The arms, not the patients, are further divided into groups according to the number of grade 4 muscles available distal to and including the brachioradialis. Since my approach is the same as given in this book, no detailed comments on it are necessary. The cases are on a more proximal neurological level than the great majority of those reported in the other papers. The key grip, not the opposition grip, is the aim of surgery which follows the same lines as described here in Chapter 8. For the first time a way to restore active elbow extension by surgery is suggested and shown to be useful. The number of hands operated on was 40 in 33 patients and 15 arms were given active elbow extension. No functional loss occurred. For six hands and one elbow extension no improvement was obtained. This book contains an expansion of the principles with additions on technique and is based on experience from more cases. Other less extensive contributions should also be mentioned.

Maury et al. (1973) updated a 1968 paper with additional cases. They reported that seventeen patients with tetraplegia out of 176 had undergone reconstructive hand surgery over a twenty year period. Because three patients underwent bilateral procedures, this series represents twenty extremities. With one or two exceptions, the patients' finger extensors were graded as three to four; therefore, this series is composed predominately of patients who must be classified as cases with low tetraplegia. In thirteen of fourteen patients, a good grasp was obtained by transferring a strong pronator teres to the flexors digitorum profundi. In some cases, the brachioradialis was transferred to the flexor pollicis longus; however, with flexion of the distal joint of the thumb, the index pulp was noted to approximate the *dorsal* surface of the thumb. The authors were not convinced that this was a useful grip and they also noted that some disturbing contractures occurred.

In the report, tests with a few other transfers were noted; however, seemingly without positive results. Also, the remainder of the report is difficult, because the translation from French into English is quite misleading. The "grand pronateur" is obviously interpreted as the palmaris longus instead of flexor carpi radialis and the "petit pronateur" is interpreted as the palmaris brevis, rather than the palmaris longus. As the palmaris brevis could not have been utilized as a transfer, the translation must be erroneous.

In 1972 and in 1976, Zrubecky, who has published important work regarding the use of orthotic and myoelectric appliances in the patient with tetraplegia, published the results of his surgical series. His approach differs from previous workers in two respects. Firstly, he performs surgery only when a useful grip cannot be obtained in other ways; and secondly, he utilizes surgery only in the nondominant hand. In order to strengthen the natural flexor hand grip, he shortens the tendons of the flexor digitorum profundi and the flexor pollicis longus. In spite of the fact that their hands had obtained additional strength, only nine of the fifteen patients reported that they were "satisfied" with the above procedure. Tenodeses for opposition of the thumb and for other purposes were performed, but no details were revealed. The total number of operations performed was 45. Zrubecky obviously feels that the field of reconstructive upper extremity and hand surgery on tetraplegia patients is quite limited.

Dolphin (1970) reported six cases in a paper given to the American Society for Surgery of the Hand. Only a review has been published but the author has kindly let me have part of the manuscript. For true opposition he uses an original method, totally different from all others. From the fused metacarpophalangeal joint of the thumb he constructs one bridle, made from the extensor pollicis brevis tendon, to the distal part of the second metacarpal and another, made from the extensor pollicis longus, to the distal end of the ulna across the palm. When the wrist extends this "sling" construction will pull the thumb in opposition against the two radial fingers. They will flex as the flexor digitorum profundus tendons are tenodesed proximally to the radius and, in order to prevent clawing, to the basal phalanges, either to the fibrous tendon tunnel or to the bone.

A follow-up study of this unpublished work was brought to my attention by the author himself. It includes six cases. In each of them only one hand was operated on. Three cases were followed up, respectively 48, 60 and 72 months after surgery. They had useful pinching and good release functions. However, a more detailed analysis of the results is not available for this very unorthodox approach – the only procedure so far which seems able to produce true opposition.

In a short paper Curtis (1974) describes his own method of treatment. It was used in ten to twelve cases (personal communication). He uses Zancolli's system of classification and his treatment is also very similar. However, Curtis does not arthrodese the thumb carpometacarpal joint, but instead choses to stabilize the distal thumb joint. In patients who have only elbow flexors and brachioradialis this muscle is used for wrist extension and the tendons of flexor pollicis longus and digitorum profundus are tenodesed to the radius. Attempts to achieve some "opposition" with a free tendon graft, also activated by wrist extension, were tried. When more function is present two separate procedures are used, one for the extensor and the other for finger flexor transfer, taking brachioradialis usually to flexor pollicis longus and extensor carpi radialis longus to flexor digitorum profundus. If still more function is available and clawing must be prevented he suggests methods described by Riordan (1974), Brand, Boyes or Fowler, with passive or dynamic use according to the needs of the case. It is clear that Curtis' cases belong more to the lower injured groups whose patients have better residual function.

The most interesting point from the Curtis' paper is his solution to the problem of determining the power of the extensor carpi radialis brevis. He opens the tendon sheath under local anesthesia at wrist level and checks the power of each of the wrist extensors separately before transferring the longus tendon, thus avoiding a disastrous mistake (p. 28).

Comments on the Literature

As mentioned before, available reports do not present a storehouse of comparable data. However, a few important facts can be extracted for further work.

1. Some surgical help can be given to many more patients than has been hitherto realized, although the results should not be exaggerated. Some important functional improvements can be made on patients with higher levels of injury. It may be that the gains made in cases at this level are limited, but Sterling Bunnell's remark retains its value "if you have nothing, a little is a lot".

2. The thumb grip is the most important, especially as useful sensibility is often left only in the thumb. It is a mistake to try giving the patients opposition, except for a very few cases with a low lesion. This is not a good grip in tetraplegia. Where are we to find all the stabilizers necessary so that index and middle fingers can counteract a strong thumb in opposition? The aim must be a *key grip, and this must be clearly emphasized, which means that adduction is the important movement to reconstruct.* Adduction was usually achieved when the aim was said to be opposition.

3. The thumb pinch obtained by tenodesis in cases where good wrist extension was the most distal residual function was regularly stronger than that obtained by musculotendinous transfer in other cases, where much more function was present. In my cases, too, tenodesis thumbs were stronger than the ones reconstructed with a more complicated technique as for example the Zancolli method.

4. With the technique now available, a flexor-extensor *finger* function will be possible only in cases better than those described here as OCu:1 and most OCu:2 cases. This requires enough residual function to give a fair finger flexor, a fair finger extension and adequate proprioception if a severe contracture is to be avoided in the long run.

5. In spite of its good anatomical position, the extensor pollicis brevis tendon, is usually too tiny to be used.

6. Arthrodesis should be avoided whenever possible.

7. Some spasticity is not necessarily a contraindication to surgery.

8. Extensor tenodesis will easily slacken in time because of lack of proprioception and protective sensibility.

9. Fingers must remain soft and flexible for human contact. Procedures such as arthrodesis or tenodesis, which put fingers into the position of fixed flexion, are rarely accepted by the patients in spite of improved gripping function. This is also the case with surgery which impairs the patient's ability to transfer or to move a wheelchair.

10. Simple procedures are the best and those which include several phases should be avoided if possible. Except for the few patients who have many muscles available, all resources should be brought together in one strong action. However, if an extensor function can be added, this is valuable especially for the fingers, less so for the thumb.

3

Anatomy, Physiology and the Loss

Reconstructive surgery of the hand includes more than the restoration of parts crippled from direct trauma. In tetraplegia the fundamental structures of the hand remain intact but the functional loss is enormous. Basic changes are needed in our thinking as the older methods of evaluation are no longer applicable to this aspect of hand surgery. The physiological state of the tissues and the neurological deficits present require a more accurate method of evaluation. Different concepts are necessary to achieve better results. The approach to every case of reconstructive hand surgery begins with an evaluation of the loss of function. What is the difference between a normal hand and the hand of the tetraplegic (Table 1), which might look fairly normal structurally?

Table 1. The loss of function in the hand of the tetraplegic

	Normal Hand	Hand of a Tetraplegic
Ligaments reliable for stabilization	45	3 (?)
Muscles available for hand motion and transfer	37	1 – 2 – 3 (?)
Tactile gnosis	Normal	Greatly reduced or absent
Proprioception	Normal	Greatly reduced or absent

My experience in this field indicates that, in order to understand the basic problems, the hand surgeon must develop his own concepts of the neurological deficits and the physiological changes. I will try to demonstrate these problems in a simple way.

Joint Ligament Action

The complicated functional structure of the normal hand is schematically built on five rays, each of them subdivided into three segments, stabilized upon each other and movable against each other within certain limits. Three segments in each one of the five rays means there are 15 segments to be stabilized. To stabilize just one such segment requires at least three stays – compare the support of a flagpole or the shrouds and stays of a mast (Fig. 1). If on the top of one segment one wishes to stabilize another segment, three more stays are required and so on. Thus, in order to stabilize the five rays in the hand, 45 stays are required and still mobility is not attained. In the hand there are two collateral ligaments and one volar plate to stabilize each joint, which means 45 stays or ligaments for the whole hand.

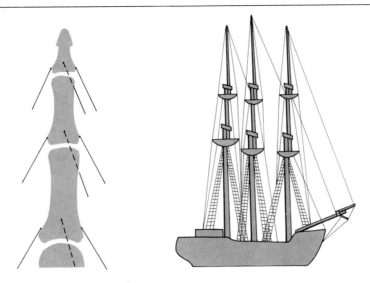

Fig. 1   To stabilize a finger every segment requires at least three stays, the ligaments. Compare the shrouds and stays of a mast

To add mobility to this system requires at least one flexor and one extensor for each joint. Other motors have been added to obtain a more complicated thumb action. In the fingers, through the ingenious construction of the dorsal aponeurosis, which in fact is a gearbox, the required number has been reduced. Thus there are 37 motors, including those for the wrist joint. The exact number depends on how the interossei and thenar muscles are counted. A glance at the incapacitated hands here in question shows five almost normal looking rays, if they have not become contracted through neglect or ill-advised treatment. The fingers are also passively mobile in approximately the normal range. One should not be misled by these apparently normal appearing structures and led to believe that reconstructive surgery simply has to bring in some motors to restore hand function. How easy is it to think that one could provide finger flexion by a simple tendon transfer. Perhaps there are already some weak finger extensors present or a tenodesis might replace them? Could not an opponens muscle from somewhere be the little thing which would make the whole hand almost normal again, etc.? How easy it is to believe that after such an operation the hand will remain like that. Undoubtedly this approach to the problem is a grave underestimation of the functional loss. The bones will decalcify to some extent, but as a rule their integrity remains adequate over a long time. This is also true of the cartilagenous structures. But what about the stays, the ligaments? Even though they may appear to be normal, can they truly be trusted? In my experience they either soften and rapidly strech out, totally losing their functional integrity (Fig. 2) or they take part in forming a severe contracture. As a matter of fact, in many patients it is easy to predict not only that they will do so but also approximately how soon this will occur. Only under a few circumstances, which are easy to identify, can the ligaments be trusted. One has,

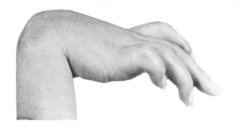

Fig. 2 In tetraplegia contractures also occur late. This hand was still useful five years ago, fifteen years after the accident. The patient could feed himself and write. Because of the tone in paralyzed muscles and lack of proprioception the ligaments have given way and the hand is totally useless. (Reprinted, by permission, from: Moberg, E.: J. of Hand Surgery I; 1, 1976)

therefore, usually very few of the 45 stays left as a base for the intended reconstruction.

There are some ligaments which will last better than others, even under adverse conditions. Best of all is the "hook" ligament at the carpometacarpal joint of the thumb. This ligament is very strong, as in a normal thumb it must resist the heavy dislocating forces of the strong abductor pollicis longus and the short thenar muscles. This ligament is actually the mechanical factor behind the Bennett fracture, as it stays intact when the bone ruptures.

Other important and almost always reliable ligaments providing lateral stabilization are the collateral ligaments of the metacarpophalangeal joints of digits II to V. Ulnar drift hardly ever occurs in the hands in question. This deformity, seen so frequently in rheumatoid arthritis, is generated by strong pull on the dislocated extensor and flexor tendons and by the hypothenar muscles, particularly the action of the abductor digiti minimi. But in these paralyzed hands the proximal phalanges stabilize each other in the lateral direction and the long muscle-tendon systems are too weak to cause lateral displacements. If the long muscles are functioning at all, they pull in a central direction, and the hypothenar muscles are often without any effect. Thus the collateral ligaments of the metacarpophalangeal joints of the fingers can be trusted. This certainly does not apply to the volar plates, which are often quite unable to prevent the most extensive joint displacement (Fig. 2). The volar plates are often too weak to be used as a basis for surgical stabilization procedures. As will be seen later, the function of the ligaments in tetraplegia can only rarely be replaced by bony fusion or other stabilization of the joints.

Muscle Action

Instead of the 37 efficient muscles acting on the normal wrist and hand, some 85 % of patients suffering from tetraplegia have lost all of the muscles active in the hand together with most wrist motors. The number of muscles present goes up to the number of the fingers on one hand only in 10 to 15 % of the cases and their power is usually also reduced. The very small percentage which have more motors left (Table 2, p. 34) also retain many of the other features necessary for hand function. Only tactile gnosis and proprioception will be mentioned here; further details will be discussed later. From the practical point of view the functions in these patients' arms are so much better that surgery is less necessary, although even here hand function often can be considerably improved.

What remains to replace this enormous loss of muscle function, to power this apparently structurally normal hand? Only very few motor functions can be replaced by tenodeses. The number of motors which could be transferred to act in the hand is rarely more than one or two compared with the 37 mentioned before. More often than not even these few are not normal. They may be either too weak to be useful or perhaps even too strong to be used without risk of later severe contracture. This raises the basic question, why the hand of the tetraplegic cannot regulate muscle power and avoid contractures in the same way as the normal hand, which has flexors three times stronger than its extensors.

Afferent Impulses

No mechanical construction, and certainly not the hand of the tetraplegic, can work without adequate information. This comes from the afferent impulses. In the ordinary problems of hand reconstruction, the importance of afferent impulses is rarely discussed. Their presence is taken for granted and indeed can be taken for granted, except for one aspect-exteroception. This is usually included in the term sensation or "feeling." Another aspect of exteroception is discussed in hand prosthetic work as "sensory feedback." This term is based on an erroneous conception and implies that motor function is the starting function, which turns the problem upside down. Every motor function and also every gripping function, whether with a hand or with a prosthesis, is just an answer to afferent impulses. The driver *sees* a car coming which he must yield to and his resultant *motor action* comes as a "feedback." Dancing couples *hear* the music and their bodies *move* as a "feedback." Every *useful* motor action (athetosis is not useful) is an answer, a response, or in other words, a "feedback" to afferent (often sensibility) impulses.

In hand surgery it is important to distinguish between two totally different functioning levels by which motor action can be instituted and controlled. Both levels are indispensible for every controlled activity. They are (1) the conscious level, for decision and learning; (2) the "computer" level, for skill and speed.

The second level of information is, as Granit says, "private to the muscles;" the person is totally unaware of it. Everyone has experienced how difficult learning can be. For example, in learning to ride a bicycle, the complex actions must be based on decisions made on the conscious level, but later they can be performed by the now trained, i.e., programmed computer system with the necessary skill and speed. Still, from time to time, for example, when a car is approaching, the conscious mind can and will interfere with the orders to the computer level for another complicated action. In the meantime the conscious level, which is the driver, is free to participate in an interesting conversation with somebody at his side.

The afferent impulses of interest in hand surgery arrive via visual pathways (rarely the auditory system) and through different kinds of sensibility. This is divided routinely into exteroception and proprioception. Regarding vision, it is only necessary to mention what is often forgotten, that is, that vision can lead to the control of one hand only at a time, never to both at the same time. This is equally true of a sensory deficient hand of the tetraplegic, stroke hand or a prosthesis.

Exteroception

The laymans term for this function is usually "feeling." This term is also used widely when patients are examined and will so continue to influence the surgeons thoughts in reconstructive work. This term, however, in hand surgery encompasses far too much and distinguishes hardly anything. It is closely connected with the need of the neurologist to separate different pathways in the medulla and with his division of "feeling" into four modalities (see also Chapter 4). He needs to know from the periphery what is wrong centrally, i.e., he goes upstairs. Reconstructive surgery, however, goes downstairs. It has a totally different problem to solve, which is to find out how useful the sensibility of the hand is for the work it has to perform and how the remaining parts can be used in the reconstructive work. It should be obvious that the concept and the tools for this kind of work must be totally different from that of the neurologist. For reconstructive surgery "feeling" is a totally useless term, as it covers far too much and distinguishes hardly anything. At one end of the scale (Fig. 3) feeling represents a valuable function. It can supply that part of the hand where it is present enough information to let it do its work without assistance from the eyes – in this case, feeling has the quality of *tactile gnosis*. But at the other end of the scale the same term "feeling" also covers the useless and harmful sensory functions, known under many different names as hyperesthesia, paresthesia, "unhappy feeling," etc. Sometimes this reaction is more "sensitive" than tactile gnosis, i.e., with lower threshold but with an abnormal response. It may be able to give some protection, for example against burns. However, while it can prevent a burn from being deep, the reaction is much to slow to prevent superficial damage. This "feeling" must be sorted out from the one which can lead and control hand function, the really useful one. How useful are parts of the hand functionally whose main role is that of being protected?

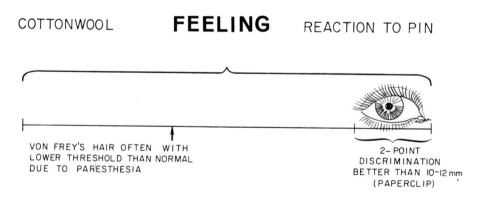

COTTONWOOL   **FEELING**   REACTION TO PIN

VON FREY'S HAIR OFTEN WITH
LOWER THRESHOLD THAN NORMAL
DUE TO PARESTHESIA

2-POINT
DISCRIMINATION
BETTER THAN 10-12 mm
(PAPERCLIP)

Fig. 3 "Feeling" covers the whole scale of sensory qualities. To the right is tactile gnosis, the high quality sensibility, which is "putting eyes" on the finger tips. Tactile gnosis is needed to allow a hand to be independent of sight. In the middle is the lower quality, which is good only for some protection. To the left is hyperesthesia or paresthesia which often destroys gripping function. The tests with a pin or cottonwool cannot distinguish between these different qualities and, therefore, are of no use in hand surgery. (Reprinted, by permission, from: Moberg, E.: J. of Hand Surgery I: 1, 1976)

The most important part of hand exteroception and the only part worthwhile registering for useful function is the tactile gnosis, the high quality function which will let fingers and other parts of the hand *see* what they are doing.

For examination of useful sensibility in reconstructive hand surgery, of all the tests evaluated by the author, the only one which was found to be significant is the two-point discrimination test now performed with a paper clip. All other tests for sensory function, in my opinion, should in this work be abandoned, including cotton wool and paper strip, pin prick, ordinary tuning fork, the difference between sharp and blunt, figure writing, the wrinkling skin test and the two-point discrimination test performed with sharp pointed compass. They are not only useless, they are even misleading.

Proprioception

An important factor rarely considered to be important in routine hand surgery is proprioception. Usually its presence is taken for granted, but this cannot be done in the type of patient discussed here. Proprioception *is* very important. It includes the conscious control of position, motion and power. There is also a "computer" control of these functions which always remains at the unconscious level, but all too often even this is lost. The patients must, after operation, program an entirely new mode of action and, therefore, must have afferent impulse up to consciousness.

To understand the role of this complicated system in surgery of the hand and to find the proper indications for the reconstruction in question, it is necessary to know about the peripheral receptors for afferent signals. The usual teaching since the days of Goldscheider (about 1890) is that the proprioceptive afferents from the limbs to the conscious level come from receptors in the joints and not from any of the cutaneous receptors. However, according to experimental work by myself and others (Moberg 1972, 1978, Grigg et al. 1973) the role of the joint receptors as the *sole* system in proprioception must be considered disproven. Contrary to the old opinion, it has been shown that skin receptors alone can provide excellent proprioceptive information to consciousness.

One important practical conclusion from this investigation is that the useful test for tactile gnosis, discussed above, also is the test for proprioception. The two-point discrimination test is the basic tool of examination. In this way proprioception can be examined for each digital segment and the results given in numerical values. Another important conclusion must be that, where the two-point discrimination shows values greater than about 10 to 12 m, cutaneous sensibility for learning and control is absent and only visual afferents remain. As vision can control only one hand grip at a time, the lack of cutaneous afferents on both hands will permit reconstruction of a useful grip in only one hand. This will be the preferred hand, if all other criteria for reconstruction are fulfilled. If, however, one hand has sensibility of sufficient quality to provide the necessary afferent impulses, both for exteroception and proprioception, then the visual control will be sufficient for surgical work on the other.

Contractures

There is another area where proprioception is important. The severe, slowly developing deformities (Fig. 2) have already been mentioned. They are found too in hands where just a minimum of active muscle power or only muscle tone remains. No strong muscle power need be present, but if present it increases the risk. It is often assumed that some imbalance in muscle power is the cause of such contractures. But power is not everything.

In the normal hand the marvellouns control of position, motion, and power applied to gripping and fine movements is based on the proprioceptive function of the afferent impulses. In tetraplegia such afferents are lost more or less completely. In the stroke hand and the cerebral palsy hand even fewer afferents usually remain. Similar deformities are rarely seen in poliomyelitis. In these patients the necessary information remains; a tendon transfer may cause a certain imbalance and still not result in a contracture. In the tetraplegic, the stroke hand, and the cerebral palsy hand the preoperative examination of the patient must determine whether proprioception is present and then reconstruction has to be planned accordingly. It must be remembered that the muscle-tendon unit will *not* provide such proprioception by itself. There is no "muscle sense in man."

How the examination and the evaluation of the cutaneous signal system are performed, is described in detail in Chapter 4.

I have tried to show how much more these hands have lost in the way of essential functions than a superficial examination will reveal. Obviously the reconstructive plan must be based on an evaluation different from the one used in most other hand surgery. Lack of understanding of this will explain why some procedures previously tried or recommended have failed. We should realize also that there may be a number of basic control mechanisms not yet discovered. As more basic facts become understood, surgery will hopefully be able to avoid the mistakes of today and be able to evaluate the functional loss of the hand of the tetraplegic as it really is.

4

Examination of the Patients for Upper Limb Reconstructive Surgery

Almost every center where tetraplegic patients are treated has its own way of examining the patients, and its own printed scheme. Usually they are very satisfactory for their purpose even if they differ in detail. As always in medicine, they have had to concentrate on what was of practical use. When reconstructive surgery becomes an important factor in the treatment, new information must be collected and recorded. This chapter will leave out most of the details already on other schemes, but offers a new way of tabulating important information for reconstructive surgery of the upper limbs. The chapter will omit discussion about such factors as the weight of the patient, motivation and psychology, or unusual systemic complications, etc. Every center with experience has good specialists available for these important matters.

The examination of the patient's upper limbs for the first time by a trained examiner usually takes about $1^1/_2$ hours. It should always take place with the patient in a wheelchair. No reliable study of hand function can be obtained with the patient in bed or on a stretcher. For the examination a scheme has been adapted especially for the evaluation of arm-hand function for surgery or splinting (Fig. 4a und b). Often this scheme is insufficient and many more details may have to be examined and listed. At the examination, it is useful if the patient brings his splints with him, the tools he uses for eating, the items he uses for daily grooming and any other special equipment. If he is able to drive, the examination will include inspection of the modifications made to his vehicle. The indications for surgery will vary according to the needs of the patient. This first examination, which is the basic one in the planning of surgery, will have to be followed by several more discussions with the patient. Very often the plan, which appeared straightforward to the surgeon after the first examination, may have to be changed after further discussions with the patient. He may bring up points of view for the functional aspect very different from the way his surgeon thinks, but of paramount importance to him. The surgeon should never try merely to make the hand resemble more closely a "normal" one. For example, a severe hand and finger contracture may be the basis for this patient's ability to drive his specially equipped car and a "correction" of his deformity may be disastrous for the patient's independence. This stresses the importance of my principle, that every procedure used in this surgery should be reversible or tested by a reversible procedure (p. 45).

Of course, the patient should always be checked again immediately before surgery.

Hand Surgery Evaluation (Tetraplegia)

Hospital:

Patient's name: _____

Date of examination: Born: Sex:

_____   Home address: Telephone
                                                                            number:

Examiner's signature: Ward: Doctor:

_____   Occupation before accident:
                         Occupation now, if any:

                         Date of injury: Type of accident: Car accident
                         Level of skeletal injury: Diving
                         Leading arm-hand before: Gunshot
                         Leading arm-hand now: _____

Use of wheelchair: Handdriven   Can raise seat in wheelchair?
                         Electric   Can turn over in bed without help?
                         Other   Can transfer without help from bed to wheelchair?
                                       Can transfer without help from wheelchair to car
                                       and back again?

Functional C level: Eating with?   Grip?   Tools?

Right   Left   Method of grooming? (Shaving, make-up)

                                       Method of writing?

                                       Stabilization in wheelchair?

Contractures?
Previous amputations?
Unusual lack of joint stability?

Group: Right   Left

       [O] [Cu] : [ ]   [O] [Cu] : [ ]

       Tr [ ]   Tr [ ]

Delete as necessary.

Name:

Spasticity (significant)	Shoulder	Wrist
	Elbow	Hand

Muscles available:
(Highets scheme)

	Right	Left
Trapezius		
Latissimus dorsi		
Deltoid		
Serratus anterior		
Rotators out		
Rotators in		
Pectoralis muscles:		
Sternoclavicular part		
Costal part		
Triceps		
Biceps + Brachialis		
Brachioradialis		
Radial carpal		
extensors (together)		
Pronator		
Finger extensors		
Long thumb abductor		
Thumb extensor		
Flexor carpi radialis		
Flexor pollicis longus		
Extensor carpi ulnaris		
Finger flexors		
Intrinsics		

Passive range of flexion
Thumb metacarpophalangeal
joint in degrees:

   R   L

Patient's understanding:

Cooperation expected:

Sensibility: (only two-point discrimination
test with paperclip of value;
includes proprioception)

	R.	L.
Thumb pulp		
Index		
Middle		
Ring		
Little		
Dorsal radial area		
Dorsal ulnar area		

Unusual features and remarks:

Patient's main hand and arm problems:

Suggestions for improvement by splinting or
surgery:

Fig. 4   Scheme for evaluation of tetraplegic patients for reconstructive upper limb surgery

Sensibility

The majority of the patients have had their sensibility examined many times before. They turn their heads away and expect to be asked whether they feel a pinprick and then, if they can differentiate between sharp or dull. It is therefore necessary to explain to them that now it is not a question of "feeling" or of "dull" and "sharp". One must emphasize to the patient the importance of the sensory examination being performed and that the result will affect the plan of the reconstructive surgery which can be offered to them, and its outcome. The patient must also be told that just "feeling" is of no interest here. Only special qualities count.

So far sensory function in the hands of the tetraplegic has only been briefly mentioned in earlier literature in this field (except in my paper in 1975). Neither the way of examining sensibility nor its major role in the indications for surgery has been discussed. The same can be said about its role in preventing contractures. It must be emphasized that sensibility together with other afferents is, in my opinion and according to my experience, the basis for reconstructive work. Sensibility can never be replaced by mechanical or other devices.

As has been stated earlier (Chapter 3) no useful grip can be obtained without sufficient afferent impulses. Not more than one hand grip can be controlled by vision alone. If there is sufficient motor function, the decision as to whether it is possible to give a patient one or two useful gripping hands will depend on the result of this sensory examination. It must be made clear right at the beginning that the methods routinely used in neurology for examining the four modalities as well as proprioception are of no use in the evaluation for reconstructive surgery. They were worked out long ago for a quite different purpose. A prominent British neurologist, Sir Russell Brain, said "the neurologist is concerned with sensibility primarily for the purpose of localising lesions in the nervous system and determining their nature." These methods of investigation are, therefore, more "rough and ready and have been adopted on account of their practical value for his immediate purpose." The neurologist's test can help to distinguish, for example, between lesions localized in different pathways in the medulla. The surgeon's purpose when examining the hand of a tetraplegic, however, is different. He must establish the value of remaining afferents for gripping and other functions and so his methods, too, must be different. Thus, the pinprick method, the cotton wool wisp, paper strip touching, differentiation between sharp and blunt, the von Freys hair, the tuning fork, the two-point discrimination test with a sharp compass, and the wrinkling skin test must be abandoned as useless or even misleading. This applies to every reconstructive hand surgery and to most other orthopedic surgery (Moberg, 1962, 1976), but has turned out to be even more true in tetraplegic hand surgery.

In the examination of sensibility for the reconstructive hand surgery and especially in tetraplegia, the only method which I have found to be useful is the two-point discrimination test. This test was developed by Weber early in the 19th century, but used by neurologists mainly for evaluation of the parietal lobe. I reported its value for hand surgery in 1962. Some modifications are necessary.

The use of sharp instruments (compass and calipers) was replaced by the blunt ends of an unfolded paperclip (Moberg 1968, 1976). The weight of the compass and caliper causes greater deformation than is acceptable, and therefore stimulates a larger area than appropriate. Sharp points easily induce hyperesthesia, especially when the instrument is used for the evaluation of results after nerve surgery, but also in some cases of tetraplegia. Therefore, sharp points make the examination unreliable and unpleasant. The use of paper-clips eliminates the shortcomings in the evaluation of the two-point discrimination test. A common small paper-clip has a diameter of 0.9 mm and the ends of the wire cut squarely, therefore eliminating the sharp ends. The paper-clip is easily available and inexpensive (Fig. 5).

Fig. 5 The unfolded paper-clip used for examination of tactile gnosis and proprioception

The examined limb and also the examinier's hand must rest against something stable, for example, a table or the armrest of a wheelchair. This is to prevent disturbing the motion of the patient's digit or the examiner's hand. The pressure applied should be minimal, hardly enough to cause a small anemic ring. In the use of this test most mistakes are made by applying too much pressure which can completely change the result (Fig. 6). More pressure will bring in more receptors in the field of stimulation, together with the increased deformation of the skin and, especially in a finger, the impression soon intrudes in the field of other nerves which may have normal receptors and normal function. This is often the case when the result of a nerve suture or a nerve graft to a single digital nerve is examined. In such cases no reliable result of the two-point discrimination test can be obtained without blocking the other three nerves in the same digit by a local anesthetic. In tetraplegia the often extensive lack of sensibility, however, is acting as a protection against such misinterpretations.

There is hardly any important difference from a functional point of view if the two-point discrimination test is performed longitudinally, obliquely, or transversely. Such variations in themselves produce results differing by little more than one millimeter. Remember also that in normal hands the nerve supply shows important variations. Six millimeters on the pulp of the thumb or the little finger after nerve surgery does not necessarily mean recovery of the median or volar ulnar nerve supply. It could mean an unusual overlap variation of the normal nerves from

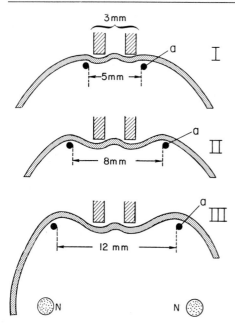

Fig. 6 Look at the skin when using the two-point discrimination test! The pressure applied is crucial. With pressure increased from I over II to III, the field of cutaneous deformation to the finger tip increases considerably and receptors more and more peripheral will be stimulated, giving rise to erroneous results. The pressure should just barely, if at all, blanche the skin. I = right amount of pressure; II and III = too much pressure; a = receptors stimulated; N = digital nerves. (Reprinted by permission, from: Moberg, E.: J. of Hand Surgery I: 1, 1976)

the dorsal side. Again a nerve block is necessary here if one really wants to trust the results obtained, but this addition is hardly ever needed in tetraplegia.

Normally variations in results occur due to the thickness of the pulp epidermis, but these will rarely exceed two millimeters and so they are practically of negligible importance. Training seems of importance as it can bring down normal two-point discrimination to about half of its previous level. Blind Braille readers can bring index finger two-point discrimination down to about 1.3 mm.

If no cutaneous surface in the examined hand has a two-point discrimination of at least 10 to 12 mm (normal is 3 to 5 mm) the afferent cutaneous impulses are not good enough to control a single hand motor grip. However, if the thumb, but not the index finger, has this sensibility a one-shank sensory grip is possible. This is inferior to the two-shank sensory grip, but is still useful. If cutaneous afferents are insufficient and vision is already occupied by the leading hand, it will not be worthwhile to consider reconstruction of the other hand. So far I know only a single exception to this rule (Case 14, p. 77 and Table 7).

In the majority of cases the examination has to concentrate on the first interspace, between the thumb and the index finger. As already mentioned, great variation occurs not only between different cases but between the right and left hand even if motor function is found to be almost identical.

Another simple method of examination has been used but given up, as the results were found to be of little or no practical value. It is the examination of the first interspace between thumb and index finger with a metal knife handle or a similar object. The blindfolded patient tries to identify the object when it is brought into this interspace, even in cases where two-point discrimination was absent. The results of this test, even if identification was sometimes possible, could never change the indications for surgery or for follow-up training.

Now that it has been shown that proprioception (the recognition of position, motion, and pressure applied) is provided to a significant amount by cutaneous receptors, the examination turns out to be exactly the same as for the sensory function discussed above. The method described with its results will also give the necessary information for proprioception. Proprioception can now be tested and the results given segment by segment with numerical values. How much joint receptors contribute is still unknown (see also the chapter on contractures).

Motor Function

For grading muscle power the widely accepted system based on the Highet scale is used (Medical Research Council 1954) in one of its variations:

0. Complete Paralysis
1. Flicker of contraction
2. Contraction only with gravity eliminated
3. Contraction against gravity only but through full range of mobility
4. Contraction against gravity and some resistance
5. Normal power.

The grades $2^1/_2$, $3^1/_2$, and $4^1/_2$ have been found useful even if they are not easily defined. This scale for muscle testing will fulfill the necessary requirements for more proximal parts of the body, but is less valid when it is applied to parts which have very little weight of their own, such as the hand and the digits. When a triceps muscle in the arm can just extend an elbow against the weight of the forearm and the hand through the whole amplitude, this means *useful* function – grade 3. When, however, a *digit* can be flexed against its own little weight, this does not mean useful function of the finger and its value corresponds to no more than grade 1 or 2 for a shoulder muscle. Therefore, the evaluation scheme must be modified when it comes to grading of wrist and digit motors. If one commences with grade 5 as the normal power and proceeds downwards on the scale, it will not be too difficult to grade the muscle from the functional point of view, comparable to that applied to a proximal muscle. This will mean that a weak but still useful muscle will be graded power 3, while 4 will mean a power between 3 and the normal 5. It is easy to raise objections from a theoretical point of view against such a loose classification of muscle power. In practical work, however, it will rarely give rise to misunderstanding, especially in tetraplegia where but few patients have motors for digits which can be graded between 3 and 5.

However, this should not lead to the belief that an examination according to a scheme will give a true picture of motor function. One only has to mention factors such as central control, speed, endurance, independence, spasticity, and athetosis, to be aware of all the difficulties and to see how limited our tests are. Especially in tetraplegia, slow sometimes creeping muscle action, easy to compare with the other side is an absolute contraindication to reconstructive surgery. So far, there is no terminology to describe the whole of this subject with the pathophysiology involved. Only lengthy descriptions are of any use. So much has to be collected in the very inconclusive and indeterminate field where testing must be substituted by what is called "clinical experience." The author has had very little help in this field from electrophysiology as it is not possible to obtain information about the power available.

As the examination of muscles is so well covered in readily available manuals, the following discussion will be limited to the few areas where mistakes are common or matters are encountered relevant to reconstructive surgery.

Three muscles form the key to the future or the present ability of the patient to raise his seat from the wheelchair, to transfer independently from bed to wheelchair and, if possible, to a normal car from the wheelchair. They are the trapezius, the latissimus dorsi, and the pectoral muscles.

The *trapezius* muscle is always present and has been good in all my cases, even in its very important distal part, which goes far down the back to the spinous process of T 12.

The *latissimus dorsi* is the biggest muscle one has to examine for reconstructive surgery. It is still the most difficult muscle of all to be assessed properly. It is the only muscle in tetraplegia which goes down the whole way to the crest of the pelvis, and if it is functioning it can play an important role in stabilizing the back. If not (and in 125 patients with tetraplegia examined by myself, it was useful, grade 3 only in 23 cases), the patient usually has to stabilize himself by hooking his nonleading arm behind the handle of the wheelchair. This observation (Fig. 8) gives the simplest clue to rule out the presence of a useful latissimus muscle. This, too, is of great importance for hand function as this particular use of the nonleading hand too often prevents its use in a two-hand grip.

If one wants to test the muscle itself, it is helpful to remember the name the old anatomists used: the musculus scalptor ani, e.e., the muscle which is used to scratch oneself in the behind. The test, therefore, is to let the patient put his hand in this position and to keep it there. The examiner tries to move it away and can get some information about its power. At the same time the examiner can get a grip around the axillary border of the muscle in front of and below the scapula with the other hand. It is interesting that this mighty muscle, when out of function in tetraplegia, "atrophies" very rapidly, much sooner than other muscles of the arm. Usually, already four to six months after the accident, only traces can be found to grip around.

In most published schemes the segments innervating the latissimus dorsi are described as C6 to C8. This does not correlate very well with the fact that this muscle rarely functions in cases where triceps, wrist flexor, and pronator teres are useful and even more distal motor functions are present. Is this lack of correspondence simply due to difficulties in evaluating the latissimus or, as I believe, should the anatomical schemes relating to this muscle be changed?

Another useful examination simultaneously tests the distal trapezius, the latissimus dorsi, and the costal part of the pectoral muscles. The examiner has to stand behind the patient, who is sitting in the wheelchair. He rests his flexed elbows in the examiner's hands and tries to raise himself from the chair. This gives a good impression of the muscle power he has available for lifting his body on extended elbows, but not for grading individual muscles. The ordinary way of testing the *serratus anterior*, by letting the patient press his hands against the wall, is not feasible in tetraplegia due to the wheelchair position. A good way to test it is in the position shown in Fig. 7 b. The patient braces his arm flexed at the elbow in the

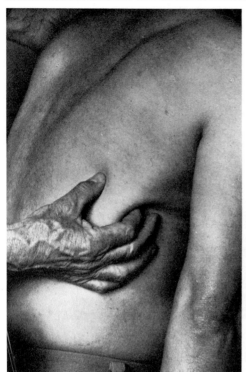

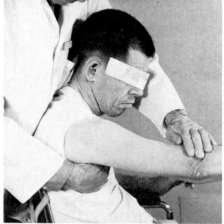

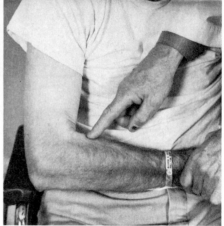

Fig. 7   The way to test a) the latissimus dorsi,
b) the serratus anterior, and c) the brachioradialis

horizontal position, and the examiner tries to push it downwards. Here it is necessary to stabilize the patient's body with the examiner's other hand on his breast.

The elbow flexors can only be tested together as one group, but it is necessary to
evaluate the power of the *brachioradialis* separately from the rest as it is one of
the most important muscles which can be used as a transfer. In fact, it is often the
only one left, but it is a difficult muscle to assess accurately. The testing must be
performed with the elbow in 90° flexion and the forearm pronated with the palm in
the sagittal plane (Fig. 7c). The examiner's hand braces the forearm whilst the
index finger of his other hand presses the bow-stringing muscle against the radius
and tries to estimate its strength. It is easy to overestimate the power, which can
be disastrous in cases where the entire reconstruction has to be built on this single
muscle acting as a wrist extensor (see also Am. case 7). Warning: I am absolutely
unable to determine whether both the *extensor carpi radialis longus* and *brevis* are
active and good. I am not able to tell whether the brevis is strong enough to be
relied upon as an only wrist extensor, especially not in cases where finger flexors
are absent – which are precisely the cases where accurate information is desired.

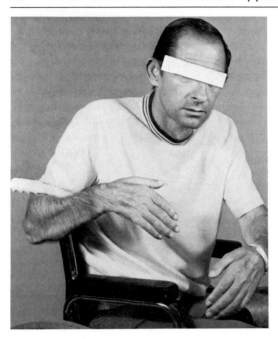

Fig. 8 When back muscles, including the latissimus dorsi, are lost, the patient usually has to stabilize himself by hooking his nonleading arm behind the handle of the wheelchair

The brevis, which is in the best position to perform wrist extension, is innervated from a lower part of the cord than the longus, and can be weak or paralyzed when the longus is good. I have seen several patients, who had been operated on earlier by other surgeons, where the longus was used as a transfer and subsequently it turned out that the brevis was not functioning. Wrist drop with total loss of wrist extension and of hand function occurred immediately. Therefore, the only way to test the brevis seems to be by making an incision over the tendon under local anesthesia and to apply a pull on it against the strong voluntary action. In four recent cases I have now performed this exploration. A straight needle was passed transversely through the explored brevis tendon. A strong thread was looped around the tendon and the needle to achieve a good hold with minimal trauma. The double thread was joined to a system of weights hanging from a cord, movable over a trundle. The result of these tests was that the brevis, if it is able to pull up and dorsiflex the wrist against a five-kilogram load over the trundle without help, can be considered good enough to work on its own as a wrist extensor. Then the longus can be made available for other purposes, for example, as a finger flexor, a thumb abductor or adductor. Only a four-kilogram force in the brevis is already reason enough to give rise to doubts. Without such a test the longus can only be used as a transfer when the functional level is obviously very much lower, i.e., in the presence of finger flexors and extensors. In such unfortunate cases where brevis failed it has been possible to perform a reconstruction with a reinsertion of the longus and reinforcement of the wrist extension with brachioradialis (Michaelis 1964, American case 4 below).

The *deltoid* muscle may be used as an elbow extensor in the reconstruction of the arm of a tetraplegic patient. To examine it, especially its posterior part, rarely raises problems. However, its existence should not be taken for granted. Cases exist where the posterior part was weak in spite of the presence of good wrist extensors in the same arm.

As will be discussed elsewhere in this book (p. 35), many unexpected variations occur in sensory and in motor functions. These may be due to incomplete lesions, to root trauma, and to the very great variety of patterns which no doubt occur in the normal anatomy of the medulla in different individuals.

5

Classification for Upper Limb Surgery

Classification of these lesions has always been a problem. When nonsurgical rehabilitation was the only treatment, classification based on the level of cord involvement could perhaps be accepted. Now that restoration of useful grip is so often feasible by reconstructive surgery, such classification is too inexact. In about half of the patients seen the degree of involvement differs in the right and left upper extremities (Table 3) and the levels of motor and sensory involvement in the same limb may not be the same. A difference of two segments, according to published schemes, is often found, and in one limb in the present series there was a difference of four segments between the levels of motor and sensory involvement. Every observer in this field knows how little the functional loss corresponds to the skeletal lesion. Therefore, if a classification is to be useful in planning treatment and comparing results of surgical procedures, it must be based on the residual functions already suggested by Lamb, Freehafer and Zancolli. It is important that the right and left upper limbs should be classified separately.

The term "incomplete" is used in many of the current schemes to explain the differences which may be found in the same hand or which may occur between the right and left hand in both motor and sensory function. For example, sometimes a strong latissimus dorsi muscle is found bilaterally in a case where grade 3 wrist extensors were the most distal muscles still useful. In the same case, sensory function in the hands came to just acceptable two-point discrimination in thumbs and index fingers. This must be explained as due to an incomplete lesion. However, this term "incomplete" is in no way helpful when indications for surgery are discussed, nor when surgical results in different hands or from different surgeons and services are compared. However valuable it may be in other fields to use classifications based on "neurological levels" or on variations of "incompleteness" in hand surgical evaluations, these terms should be abandoned as useless. A new way must be found.

Sensibility (exclusively tactile gnosis) as a guide

In the classifications proposed in the past, sensibility in the hand was occasionally mentioned but its importance was hardly discussed at all. However, voluntary grip is always a response to afferent impulses and is guided by these impulses. Normally, both vision and sensibility in the hand control the grip. But in almost every other hand operated on in my patients there was no useful sensibility at all. These patients therefore had to rely entirely on ocular afferent impulses to control grip, a condition that was a severe limitation, but the restored grip was useful none-theless.

As mentioned before, if no more than ocular afferent impulses are present, the patient has only sufficient afferents to control one hand in independent gripping functions. Useful cutaneous sensibility in at least one hand is a "must" if any attempt to restore useful grip in both hands is being contemplated.

Motor Function

Having identified the patient's resources in the way of afferent stimuli, available motor function is assessed. Only rarely can a muscle be transferred to restore grip if its rating is less than 4 by the Highet scale of 0 to 5. Any muscle considered for transfer must have power clearly superior to that necessary to lift the part against gravity (see also p. 25). In the classification to be described only grade 4 muscles are considered except when a grade 3 brachioradialis and grade 3 radial wrist extensors are present and can be combined to produce one muscle action with grade 4 power.

Among patients suffering from tetraplegia there is a very small group in whom the lesions are at levels higher than those included in the classification proposed here. These patients are the ones who make up part of Freehafer's group I (only shoulder shrug and no upper limb control), the others in his group I have elbow flexion but no voluntary function of the wrist and hand. Sometimes, however, the patients in this category have a grade 4 brachioradialis and can be included in my classification, because grip reconstruction will sometimes be feasible in them. All patients in whom surgical reconstruction of grip is not feasible are best classified according to the cord segment involved, usually the fourth cervical level or above. However, anatomical variations occur.

Author's Classification

The classification described here ignores the cord lesions and must be applied to each upper extremity. Every patient, therefore, has one classification for the right hand and one for the left hand.

The scheme of the classification also includes *two main groups* based on the afferent stimuli available to control grip: ocular only (O) and ocular and cutaneous sensibility in the hand (OCu).

Each of these main groups is broken down into eight subgroups based on the available grade 4 muscles, as follows.

Group O – Only ocular impulses are present to control gripping function:

O:0 No grade 4 muscle below elbow
O:1 Brachioradialis
O:2 Same as O:1 plus radial carpal extensors
O:3 Same as O:2 plus pronator
O:4 Same as O:3 plus flexor carpi radialis
O:5 Same as O:4 plus extensor digitorum communis
O:6 Same as O:5 plus extensor pollicis longus
O:7 Same as O:6 plus some of the long finger flexors
O:8 Same as O:7 plus intrinsic muscles of the hand.

In posttraumatic tetraplegia groups O:4 to O:8 occur very rarely or not at all, but they are seen in other diseases.

Group OCu – Ocular and cutaneous impulses present:

OCu:0 No grade 4 muscle below elbow

OCu:1 Brachioradialis

OCU:2 through OCU:8 Same as described for these subgroups in group O.

For the hands which show fewer functional defects or are near normal, descriptions in terms of loss usually will be preferable.

This classification may be elaborated by adding a grading of a triceps muscle, grades 0 to 5. This can be simplified as triceps + (plus) if the power is grade 3 or above and triceps − (minus) if less than power 3 (Table 2). This function is a consideration of importance in the plan for treatment as some active elbow extension can be restored by transfer of the deltoid and may greatly benefit the patient.

6

Statistical Survey

Very little has been reported in detail regarding the motor and the sensibility functions remaining in the upper extremities in tetraplegia. Obviously, the information obtained from classification according to functional "cervical level" is far too crude for this purpose. The variations which are found are not only of basic importance when evaluating the different cases for treatment, but also in finding out what can be done to each arm. The lack of interest previously shown for such detail is easily understood, as it did not influence the kind of treatment which could be offered.

As stated in Chapter 5 a detailed knowledge of residual motor and sensibility function is now the basis of the surgical evaluation. Statistics based on the arms examined and recorded is given here. As almost all the cases were seen by myself, this information is very uniform from a technical point of view.

The number of arms reported here is 321, of course this number is steadily going up, but so far no change in frequency between different groups has occurred. However, for a number of reasons it is obvious that these cases will not be truly representative of the total group of tetraplegica. Different survival rates among the very high lesions will influence the statistics. Almost all the patients examined were in wheelchairs and this will reduce the number of higher lesions seen, but the fact that more in-patients than out-patients are examined will act in the other direction. Many patients have come spontaneously great distances after meeting friends who have had surgery and this could have distorted the figures. Patients at the American Veterans Hospitals hospitalized for a long time have had easier access to surgery and may be overrepresented.

The figures are not divided separately for Scandinavian and American cases. The tables (2 to 4) give all the details. It is clearly seen that the large groups are the O:1, OCu:1 and OCu:2, together representing two thirds of the total. The great majority of them and altogether more than 70 % of all tetraplegics lack sufficient triceps function for reliable control of their arms in the elevated position. This is also very important when the patients are in bed. Only limbs from the group of OCu:3 and better regularly possess some useful triceps function (Table 2). In about 12 % of all arms the remaining *motor* function is so poor that it will exclude any improvement of hand function using present surgical methods. However, the fact that sufficient afferent cutaneous impulses are so often lacking (in about 40 % of the arms) will further limit this surgical help to many more hands. It must be repeated that without enough afferent cutaneous information only one of the patient's two arms can be given a single hand grip. Psychological reasons and some

Table 2. Total number of examined hands and arms grouped according to authors classification
Surgery registered possible – surgery performed

Groups	% of total	Number in group	Triceps force 3 or better	Surgery to hand registered possible	Surgery to hand performed	Surgery to elbow registered possible	Surgery to elbow performed
O:0	12	38	0	5*)	4	5	2
O:1	24	77	2	36	26	19	13
O:2	4	12	2	9	7	6	4
O:3	0.3**)	1	0	1		1	
OCu:0	2	6	2	2*)	2	2	
OCu:1	16	51	4	39	18	35	12
OCu:2	27	88	28	59	34	48	15
OCu:3	8	25	25	18	11	1	
OCu:4	2	8	8	7	6		
OCu:5	1	4	4	3	2		
OCu:6	1	3	3		1		
OCu:7	0.6**)	2	2	1	1		
OCu:8	2	6	6	3			
		321	86	183	112	117	46
			27 %	57 %	35 %	50 %***)	20 %***)

*)   Borderline cases with very weak muscles, but a trial was made
**)   Decimals given only for the smallest groups
***)   Percentage counted on the 235 arms lacking useful triceps

somatic and environmental contraindications will raise the number of patients (not arms) to about 30 – 40 % for whom no surgical reconstruction can be recommended today. I was surprised that the number of arms which are better than OCu:3 is so small, about 7 %. They are, however, the cases for whom most of the surgical approaches have been described previously. Even without surgery they often have a fairly good single hand grip and, therefore, in the early stage of my work I usually did not offer them surgical help. This was an unnecessary precaution. It has been shown by the surgeons mentioned earlier, and I have now myself the experience, that the function of these patients can be considerably improved with almost no risk and today they are offered help. Why should they be denied it when so many injured hands with much less functional loss are operated on with useful results?

The differences between both arms on the same patient are set out in Table 3. As can be seen, every second *patient* showed approximately the same loss in both arms. The other 50 % of the patients showed an obvious difference between the two arms, and frequently this was quite marked. The American and Scandinavian cases are almost the same in number and from other points of view so similar, that no details are required. However, the American group shows slightly greater differences between both arms. This is probably due to the fact that gun shot injuries did not occur among the Scandinavian cases.

Table 3. Variations between both hands on individual patients

Group for both hands if same or, if different, for nonleading side	Both sides same group	The two sides different	If different, the leading side belongs to group:											
			O:1	O:2	O:3	OCu:0	1	2	3	4	5	6	7	8
O:0	10	18	11			5	1	1						
O:1	22	22		4	1	10	5	2						
O:2	2	4					3	1						
O:3	0	0												
OCu:0	2	2				2								
OCu:1	9	16					13	3						
OCu:2	28	10						9	1					
OCu:3	3	3							1	2				
OCu:4	2	2								1				1
OCu:5	0	1									1			
OCu:6	1	1											1	
OCu:7	0	0												
OCu:8	2	0												
	81	79												

It is not discussed here how much the differences between both arms were due to anatomical variations in the medulla (and why should the medulla be more "standardized" than other parts of the nervous system?), to asymmetrical medulla lesion or to different degrees of plexus or root involvement. The differences, however, are important in planning surgery and make all attempts to produce a rigid scheme of surgical indications impossible. Still more far-reaching variations in the same arm, not shown in the tables, can be detailed here. A weak deltoid, especially in the posterior part, has been found in a patient with a good OCu:2 hand. A strong pronator of grade 3 or even 4 has been found in the absence of wrist extensors and with a weak brachioradialis. A good thumb adductor and some interosseous function has been found with very weak finger extensors and flexors. A weak brachioradialis was found with strong wrist extensors, etc. All this indicates that the tables hitherto published on segmental innervations of the muscles can be used only as a very crude guide.

Needless to say, a similarly variable picture to motor loss is found for the distribution of sensibility. One case can serve as an example. In the same arm there was a four segment difference between the sensibility and residual motor function according to standard schemes of anatomical innervation. The individual tetraplegic does not follow these schemes and the surgery to be suggested should not be influenced by them.

Table 4 shows the variations of the sensibility distribution, the tactile gnosis of the five digits in the different groups. Only the pulp sensibility is recorded in the table. In every case the regression of sensibility was from the radial to the ulnar side of the hand and there were no cases in which ulnar sensibility was better than in the thumb region. Occasionally there were exceptions to this rule on the dorsal side of the hand. There were so few cases with fields of adequate dorsal sensibility that this factor so far has no visible influence on the treatment. The table is based on the Scandinavian cases alone, but there is no significant difference in the American cases.

Table 4. Digits with tactile gnosis and proprioception in the different groups.
Only the Scandinavian cases

Group	Only thumb pulp	Also: index pulp	+ middle pulp	+ ring pulp	+ little pulp = on all digits
OCu:0	5	1	0	0	0
OCu:1	29	11	3	1	3
OCu:2	24	42	8	0	5
OCu:3	4	8	1	6	6
OCu:4			2	2	3
OCu:5				2	2
OCu:6				1	2
OCu:7					2
OCu:8					3

It should be mentioned here that careful assessment of the quality of sensibility influences the prediction of the risks of contracture, especially in cases where muscle transfers to the digits are in question. But so far no figures can be given.

The columns of Table 2 reporting the number of patients for which surgery was found advisable must be read with reservation. Very often the procedures were just registered as "found possible". These are shown in the first column of this table. In some cases further surgical indications appeared at a later date. In the early development of the work, indications for surgery were found less often than later, due to lack of experience. The figures must not be taken as a statement that the patients were recommended to have an operation. Almost always they were just told what the surgeon believed possible and the decision was left to them. Obviously many different circumstances influenced this decision. The number actually undergoing surgery is of less interest.

At the beginning very few like to try what appears to them a risky and uncertain approach. They have so little left and an unfortunate outcome would leave them almost helpless. But when the first few brave patients are freed of their plaster, the others are all around to look and soon the number of operations increases. Therefore, it is obvious that the rate of acceptance of the suggested interventions and the percentage performed is much higher in the Scandinavian group where work has gone on for years. In the American group it was a matter of a nine months period where at the end surgical facilities were limited and could not deal with all patients who wanted surgery. Quite a few of them will eventually be operated by other surgeons of the hospitals in question. A very limited number were border-line cases (Table 7) where the patients wanted an attempt to be made in spite of being told that very little was available and that the outcome might be no improvement or merely a small plus.

In other countries and under other circumstances all these figures may be different. An example can be given from Argentina. During a recent visit in 1977 to Dr. E. Zancolli in Buenos Aires we found that our ways of examining *motor* function gave comparable results. And so Table 5 could be constructed. In this table only the motor function is considered and the Zancolli figures refer to cases, whereas my own refer to arms.

Table 5. Remaining motor function. Comparison between cases of Zancolli (= Z) and Moberg (= M)

Groups	poor	Z Argentina	M Scandinavia, USA
		% of all	
Z = 5A; 5B; 6A M = O:0; O:1; OCu:0; OCu:1		26	54
Z = 6B1; M = O:2; OCu:2		43	31
Z = 6B2 + 3; M = OCu:3		18	8
Z = 7A + B; 8A + B M = OCu:4−8		13	7

better

Clearly the difference is important. In Scandinavia and the USA, many more high level cases with more severe loss will come to the surgeon. In contrast to this, the cases in Argentina have more residual muscle function. The difference may be due to lower mortality in Scandinavia and the USA among cases with a higher lesion, but this is not known. However, it explains why in this book much more interest is shown in reconstructive work for cases with a higher loss, as to my experience these cases dominate in number and need.

To summarize, despite the fact that my random grouping is not truly representative, it is interesting to see how the arm and hand factors occur overall and as separate groups. To my knowledge no similar statistical survey is available.

7

Planning for Constructive Surgery and Contraindications

From my point of view, the most difficult features of this work are to be found in evaluation before surgery and in follow-up treatment, not in the surgical procedure itself. First of all, the contraindications must be observed, but even then the surgeon still must decide on the right procedure, the right timing, the right order and the right interval between the different procedures.

Only wheelchair patients can be selected for this surgery. Surgery for pressure sores is often unpredictable in its course, and hand surgery can and always should wait its turn, but when performed only emergencies should be permitted to distract the patient's attention from his upper extremity problems.

The dominant hand should be treated first and invariably I have regretted it if the patient had talked me into starting with the other hand. Naturally, the question which hand should be treated first can only be raised if sufficient afferent impulses are left for grip construction in both hands. If they are very close to each other in sensory and motor resources, the dominant hand is often the one the patient used more before the accident, even if this hand is now, to some extent, not as good as the other. If, however, the difference is more than one step on the classification scale used here, usually the better hand should be regarded as the dominant one, even though the poor functional value of both hands before surgery makes the patient prefer the one originally more closely linked to his brain.

If the patient is cooperative, the situation is promising and the plan includes hand grip as well as elbow extensor, the surgeon is recommended to start with the elbow. If he chooses the reverse order, the patient is subjected to a boring situation. The first operation gives him a useful single hand grip, and the elbow extensor surgery then deprives him of it for at least three months just as it starts to be useful. The presence of an elbow extensor also is needed for the learning of a new function by a transferred brachioradialis muscle (p. 51). If more function remains, more complicated procedures can be suggested and performed. If the patient has less, the plan must be simplified as much as possible. This means that in the O:1 to O:3 cases, it can almost never be a question of more than a simple key grip, perhaps combined with a weak pronation procedure. As is usually the case, not only in this field, the surgeon experienced in one method will probably get the best results from the one he is accustomed to.

Quite often the patients wants to have more than one operation performed at the same time or he wants the interval between two procedures shortened. I always refuse to do the hand and the elbow at the same time. When elbow reconstruction is trained and 90° of flexion can be achieved with full active extention, I have found it possible to do hand surgery in cases where the hand procedure does not require any immobilization of the elbow. To perform surgery on both sides simultaneously, or with a short interval between two operations, leaves the patient quite helpless and adequate training is not possible.

In the ideal plan the treatment of each hand and each elbow extensor should be nearly completed before the next procedure is started. It should not be forgotten that it takes time to get a new function trained and more or less made automatic. In this field, more than in other reconstructive hand surgery, training will take longer as the afferent impulses to conscious level are almost always reduced and the endurance of the patient is diminished.

Some patients have told me that an elbow extensor can be of use even in arms where no hand surgery can be suggested. They have had one elbow operated on already and urged me to do the other one as well. Driving, propelling the wheelchair and two-hand actions have in such cases been improved and so this possibility should not be ruled out. I have learned more and more from these patients and found their views realistic.

Very often a boring time has to proceed the surgery itself. It means getting the arm and hand as free as possible from contractures. Splinting and rubberband traction requires the closest supervision by the surgeon himself (American Case 1 and Fig. 21 g).

It is of paramount importance in this surgery to reach the best possible understanding with the individual patient of what can be done and the narrow limits within which the surgeon is working. No surgeon is able to explain this to a new candidate as well as the patients can do who have already been operated. Doubtful cases should only be considered if the surgery is generally accepted at the local hospital because of a number of successfull cases. The important contraindications for surgery are the following:

1. *Patient in bed.* Just as no reliable examination can be performed no satisfactory follow-up treatment can be given to a bedridden patient. The patient cannot be trained in bed and thus no useful function can be obtained. Candidates for surgery must be mobile in wheelchairs. The simultaneous treatment of other major or minor problems should not be undertaken, except in emergency situations, until the time after surgery when the upper limb is out of plaster and training is advanced, as this requires the patient's full attention. Under no circumstances should pressure sores be treated at the same time.

2. *General inactivity.* Major psychological problems and inactivity are strong contraindications. The patient must want the operation. If he hesitates it is usually best to postpone surgery until he has met and talked with other tetraplegic patients who have already had their operation. Nothing is more difficult than a patient with too high expectations which cannot be fulfilled, he will also be a danger to other patients.

3. *Spasticity.* This can be a serious contraindication but must not always be so, as has been discussed in other chapters where spasticity has been mentioned. In a few cases it can even be helpful.

4. *Abnormal quality* of motor action is, however, always prohibitive. The slower "creeping" muscle activity for which neither tests nor terms exist so far, even if it is under voluntary control, will not produce acceptable function. Sometimes it can

be useful for the diagnosis to ask the patient to perform the same rapid motion simultaneously with both arms, if one is more normal than the other. The abnormal nature of the movement will then be obvious.

5. *Lack of adequate nursing facilities.* It must be remembered that the upper extremity is just a part of the tetraplegic patient and his problems. Bowel care, urinary problems and especially the prevention of pressure sores are even more important than usual during the period the patient has his arm in plaster. The special training and facilities for this immediate care are rarely present in a general, orthopedic or plastic surgery ward. It is usually much safer to bring the patient from the specialized long-term rehabilitation ward to surgery for the few hours needed. After the operation he can be taken back and this is safer than trying to get the necessary surgical follow-up on these other wards.

It is no contraindication to surgery if the patient is aged 60 or older, nor if the patient was injured long ago. It is a general belief that after some years patients "settle down and accept their situation" and are negative to reconstructive surgery. Of course, such patients exist, but generally this opinion is false. This attitude may come from the nursing staff or the patient himself, but it rapidly fades when he comes into contact with other patients who have already been operated on (Table 6).

Table 6. Time in years between accident and reconstructive arm and hand surgery

68 consecutive cases	
< 1 year	8
1 – 2 years	20
2 – 3 years	7
3 – 5 years	8
5 – 8 years	12
> 8 years	13
	68

(Max. 14 years, min. 7 months)

6. *Lack of continuity* in surgical work or in the follow-up work. The whole treatment must be in the hands of *one* surgeon who not only has the time and interest to attend to all the small details of examination, surgical technique, and follow-up treatment, but also the training necessary to achieve worthwhile results.

Surgery

General Principles

Of course, in this surgery the best surgical judgments of the technique are necessary because available resources for sensibility and power are very limited. Greatest care must be taken not to allow impairment of soft tissue gliding function during and after surgery. Established principles for hand surgery must be followed. A bloodless field is obvious and need not be mentioned. The same applies to what is called an "atraumatic" technique. It must be kept in mind that adhesions are formed after any surgery, even the very best, and that the tetraplegic patient has weak muscles. Therefore, he has less ability to mobilize adherent tendons and other structures. Great care must be taken to minimize adhesions and the formation of scar tissue. No tissue should be permitted to get dry and it should be kept moist by the most innocent fluid, preferably buffered Ringer's Solution. No dry sponging should be permitted and all sponging should be kept down to a minimum. Co-agulation of small bleeders is, no doubt, very useful in the deltoid transfer operations, but only a very limited use of bipolar coagulation can be permitted in hand surgery. It must be remembered that the burned areas are always much more extensive than immediately observed. Catgut, which gives more scar reaction than most other suture materials, should rarely be used. Vessels can be tied with very fine nylon or similar thread. It should be remembered that the areas of the finger nails can never be kept entirely free from active bacteria, therefore, the patient's skin should not be touched by the surgeon's hands more than is absolutely necessary. It is much safer to cover any area to be held with a sponge. Skin closure should not be tight, and space should be left for the drainage of transudate forming during the first few hours and for the unavoidable slight swelling of wound edges. As in other hand surgery, I always flush the wound after closure with the same fluid used for moistening sponges, in order to wash out as much as possible of the slight oozing of blood still present. Then the compression dressing is applied as quickly as possible. For work in the hand no drains have been used. In most deltoid transfers a medium sized suction drain has been used for one or two days.

After surgery immobilization with a plaster splint (Fig. 9a) is necessary except for very small secondary procedures. If only procedures 1 to 4 (p. 48) are performed, a well-moulded and well-padded plaster splint from below the elbow to the finger tips is sufficient. Sometimes the four ulnar digits are left outside the plaster and the compression dressing. The thumb is, of course, included and usually put in adduction and flexion in order to avoid tension on the flexor pollicis longus tenodesis. The

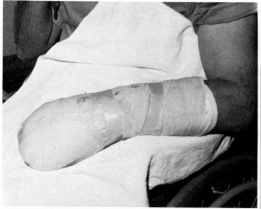

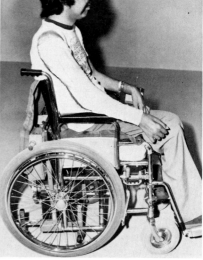

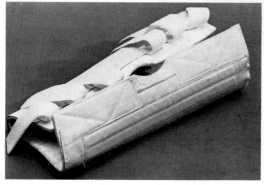

Fig. 9 a) The plaster after hand surgery, b) the patient in wheelchair with plaster three days after the elbow extensor procedure and, c) the child's knee splint for protection of the arm after removal of plaster

wrist is usually kept in slight dorsiflexion. If some swelling of the fingers is expected the four fingers are included in the compression dressing and the plaster. It must be remembered that the flow of blood and lymph from the hand in tetraplegia is very much impaired by the lack of pumping action of normal muscles. For this reason, in cases of deltoid transfer, the hand may be given a simple compression dressing for the first week. If this is not done swelling may easily occur which is much more persistent than swelling in a normal hand. When more complicated procedures are performed the different parts must be splinted in the position which gives the optimum relaxation to the tissues involved.

It should always be remembered that most of the skin surfaces in this surgery are anesthetic or have reduced sensibility. Therefore, great care is necessary to avoid pressure sores especially from the plaster, which must be well-padded. In my opinion, the surgeon should do all the plaster himself and never leave this work to helpers for whom the patient's lack of sensibility might be less obvious. I also always stay with the patient until the plaster is set.

For most of the hand procedures mentioned hereafter, the plaster was left in place with the dressings undisturbed for three weeks. Then all dressings were removed, and only rarely was a further dressing required. It should be mentioned that in cases where the wrist extensor and brachioradialis muscle only had grade 3 strength, if the immobilization was prolonged by only two or three days, there was a long delay in restoring adequate range of motion.

The general care of the patients should preferably be performed in wards especially with specially trained nurses for all the other problems in tetraplegia, not in wards for general or orthopedic surgery.

A few words should be said about how the muscles appear in the field of surgery and what this means, as some false conclusions seem to occur. Some muscles are seen to be more or less atrophied, even to the extent of just a thin fibrous lining being left of e.g. the pronator quadratus muscle. But in other cases such a muscle may have the thickness of almost half an inch and look normal in every respect. Still it may be absolutely useless. It is easy to understand that a muscle still connected with its anterior horn cells in the medulla keeps its normal appearance in this way, even if out of function for decades (Fig. 10a, b). If however, this connection is lost, either through a crush of the medulla itself or through a root or a nerve lesion peripherally to the medulla, the muscle will get more and more atrophied in time. All variations that occur are due either to more or less complete lesions or to the time factor. For the surgeon it is important to remember that, unlike most other hand surgery, in this case no positive information whatsoever can be obtained from looking at the muscles in the surgical area. A muscle, appearing to be absolutely normal, is very often dead from the functional point of view.

Fig. 10 Muscles, which are still connected to their anterior horn cells in the medulla keep (a) their normal appearance and will only be moderately reduced in size, even if they have not been functional for decades. Therefore, a linear cut through the medulla should theoretically give only a moderate reduction in the muscle mass as most of the anterior horn cells are left intact. On the other hand a crush of the medulla, a root or a nerve lesion or a combination will give an extensive loss of muscle mass (b). When such a loss is present it is generally difficult or impossible to apportion the part played by either factor

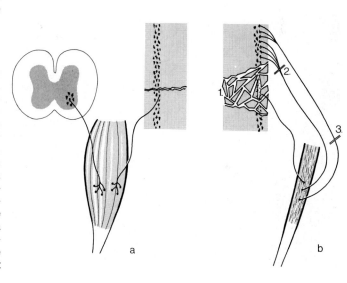

Anesthesia

In the great majority of cases, general anesthesia has been used with or without intubation. In less than twenty cases, a supraclavicular plexus block was used, always performed by myself as I have personal experience of several thousand similar blocks. Twenty milliliters of two percent xylocaine with adrenalin 1:100,000 was used. The needle was never bigger than 20 × 0.4 mm and was inserted with the cutting plane parallel to the nerve fibers. The infrequent use of this technique here differs from my practise in other hand surgery where it is used in about 95 % of all my cases. This is due to the very uncommon but not avoidable risk of paresthesia due to small intraneural hematomas persisting over a few months. For the tetraplegic patient this could greatly interfere with his training during the very important starting period.

A very good new form of axillary plexus block anesthesia has been described by Selander (1977) and it appears to be especially useful for surgery in tetraplegia. In my work it has been used only four times, always performed by the author of the method. A small, flexible, disposable intravenous catheter on a stainless steel stylet (Fig. 11) is introduced into the neurovascular sheath in the axilla and pushed up proximally. It is used for administration of the anesthetic solution, which is usually 1 % plain mepivacaine 20 to 40 ccm. If, during surgery, the anesthesia is insufficient, more can easily be added the same way. This anesthetic is free from the risks involved in the brachial plexus block previously described, it does not influence the activity of the diaphragm and can be high enough to eliminate pain from the cuff having very little influence on the patient's general condition. He can have his ordinary meals straight after surgery. However, the technique seems to require some training.

Less extensive procedures have often been performed under a radial or median nerve block.

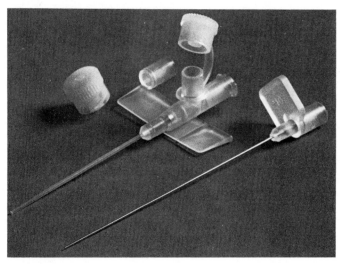

Fig. 11 The instrument for the Selander type of axillary block.

The Hand

The Aim and the Principles

The major functions of the hand can be broken down into three categories: sensory function, gripping and human contact. Any reconstructive program must aim to restore these functions as much as possible and should not under any circumstance cause any further impairment to them than they already have. The importance of sensory function and gripping is well recognized and requires no comment. The human-contact function of the hand, on the contrary, is too rarely mentioned, even though it is of paramount importance. The experienced hand surgeon knows that the majority of his patients with Dupuytren's contracture consult him because of this problem. Some have trouble shaking hands. Quite a few are sent by spouses who cannot stand their partner's clawlike hands. Tetraplegic patients usually are young men who fight desperately to keep their girl friends. Soft pliable hands are an asset, even with no active grip, and under no circumstances can be given up. Procedures to give an active grip by creating permanently flexed, more or less stiff fingers, unsuitable for human contact, will often be rejected by the patient. The use of orthoses poses the same problem. Therefore, human contact (Fig. 12) must always be considered in any plan to restore hand function by reconstructive surgery.

Fig. 12 This rock-carving was made with a stone in hard granite in Sweden some 4000 years ago. Obviously, it depicts a young couple and the artist was quite aware of the fact that hands are the most important organs for human contact. Hand surgeons of today should follow his teaching

Another basic principle that must guide the planning of treatment is the requirement that any procedure performed must be reversible. These patients are so severely handicapped that any functional loss may be disastrous. If, after surgery, the patient says, "I was better off before the operation", it must be possible to restore him to his former condition. Although this situation has not occurred in my series so far, the principle must remain inviolate even though it limits the number of procedures that may be used.

Broadly speaking, the goal of surgical treatment is to provide the patient with the ability to grip objects with one hand and to have extension of one or both elbows of sufficient strenght to stabilize the forearm in any position, or even in a few cases to make independent transfer from a bed to a wheelchair or from a wheelchair to a car possible.

To my knowledge, my approach to the restoration of grip in these patients differs from that of most previous authors. The goal of treatment is *key grip* (Fig. 24a), never tripod or thumbindex pulp pinch. Key grip is stronger, provides broader gripping surfaces, is cosmetically preferable, and is easier to achieve. It is the grip we all use in about 50 % of our gripping actions. Tetraplegic patients will not pick up needles or small nuts, but will handle newspapers, books or a piece of bread and will use the hand while dressing and doing other actions for which this grip is normal. Procedures to provide a key grip will not interfere with the functions of the hand in human contact, nor destroy the important "interlacing grip" (Fig. 24c) which is useful when there are no active finger motors. Thumb opposition is not a useful function in hands in which lack of available resources will necessitate stiffening of a number of parts in order to achieve opposition. As noted by Jackson, those who might be tempted to fix the thumb in the position of opposition should remember that this is a fantastic cost in terms of function for very little gain in activity. It should also be noted that for the majority of patients with tetraplegia at the higher levels under consideration here, reconstructive procedures on the index, middle, ring, and little fingers are not recommended. These digits must be kept soft and pliable for human contact. Only about 15 % of all patients are on a level where some restoration of finger action can be considered. The minimum requirements to restore key grip are: (1) afferent impulses, (2) one mobile joint in the thumb (the wrist joint is of course also necessary, as are proximal joints in the arm, but these joints are not really part of the grip mechanism), and (3) one motor.

The minimum afferent impulses can be provided either by vision or by cutaneous sensibility in the thumb or index finger if two-point discrimination is at 10 to 12 mm or better. If only one shank of the gripping mechanism has sensibility, the grip is always less good than the between two gripping parts, each with useful sensibility. Therefore it is very advantageous to have good two-point discrimination in both thumb and index finger. All too often, the patients in question have only ocular afferent impulses and hence only one hand can be given a grip.

The minimum motor prerequisite is a grade 3 wrist extensor system, either already present or possible, to achieve through a transfer. If the wrist extensors are present but too weak they must be reinforced by the brachioradialis. But in such cases to be effective an elbow extensor construction is also usually needed (p. 51). If they are good enough (extensor carpi radialis longus and brevis together), the brachioradialis muscle can be used in another way, for example to provide a thumb abductor.

If the wrist extensors are really strong, close to grade 5, and good thumb function is expected through adequate surgery, in some cases a finger flexion construction could be considered too. Usually the patient belongs to the OCu: 3 group or even better. Functional wrist flexor is of importance for finger extension which is achieved automatically when the wrist goes volarly. Therefore, flexor carpi radialis should *not* be used as a transfer in order to activate the finger flexors. A good brachioradialis may be used if active elbow extension is present. Under certain conditions (p. 28) extensor carpi radialis longus could also be considered for this purpose.

If still more is available as in group OCu:4 brachioradialis is useful as a finger extensor and the extensor carpi radialis longus as a finger flexor. However, this should be done as a two-stage procedure. A thumb adductor is also very useful and is an early goal for reconstructive work in cases where an abductor is left, even if it is weak.

In cases with a tendency to hyperextension in the metacarpophalangeal joints, or even advanced contracture (clawing), the Zancolli "lasso" operation (p. 56) is a very useful procedure, not necessarily requiring more than tone in the superficialis muscle.

For the patients who have hands belonging to the OCu:5 group or still better, the approach can sometimes be totally different, more similar to the solutions used in other reconstructive hand surgery. Such cases are, however, so rare and show such great variations, that no plan for treatment is required here. It should be remembered that these patients usually have ample tactile gnosis as well as proprioception.

The Basic Procedure for a Simple Hand Grip

The basic procedure (Fig. 13a,b) consists of: (1) the construction (if need be) of a wrist extensor using the brachioradialis; (2) release of the flexor pollicis longus tendon over the thumb metacarpophalangeal joint by resection or opening of the annular ligament to increase the distance between the center of rotation of the joint and the tendon, thereby increasing the mechanical advantage of the weak flexor system; (3) stabilization of the distal thumb joint with a longitudinally inserted, buried Kirschner wire; and (4) tenodesis of the flexor pollicis longus tendon attaching it to the volar surface of the radius.

After completion of these procedures, when the wrist goes into active extension the flexor tenodesis presses the thumb against the side of the index finger and the wire prevents flexion of the interphalangeal joint (Froment's sign). Wrist flexion by gravity opens the grip.

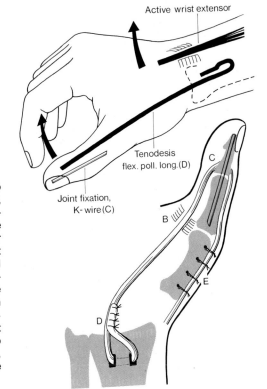

Fig. 13   The basic steps in the procedure to provide a key grip: if wrist extension is weak, the brachioradialis is transferred to the extensor carpi radialis brevis; (B) and (D) the flexor pollicis longus is tenodesed to volar surface of radius and the annular ligament at the metacarpophalangeal joint is resected to permit the tendon to bowstring and increase the strength of the key grip: (C) the thumb interphalangeal joint is stabilized with a Kirschner wire to prevent flexion (Froment's sign) and to maintain a broad contact surface; (E) if too much flexion of the thumb metacarpophalangeal joint is possible, extensor tendons are tenodesed to the metacarpal

Variations of and additions to this basic procedure are necessary, because of individual differences in the two hands of the same patient or in the hands of different patients. Detailed and repeated clinical examinations are needed to work out these variations. Every hand is a different problem just as the personality of each patient is different. The procedure mentioned so far forms the basis for the gripping function which can be obtained for the great majority of patients suitable for reconstructive surgical work.

Technical Details

Including the four basic procedures already mentioned the following have been tested in my work and may be used to restore hand grip in these patients:

1. Release of the annular ligament at the level of the metacarpophalangeal joint of the thumb to permit bowstringing of the flexor tendon, thus increasing its mechanical advantage.

Through an oblique incision the sheath fixing the flexor pollicis longus tendon at the level of the metacarpalphalangeal joint is divided. The very large digital nerves to the thumb are located very superficially here, more than in normal hands, and they are surrounded by tissues which are more fibrotic. Great care must be taken not to injure them as they are often the only nerves left in the hand on which all important afferent impulses can be based. When the nerves are located and kept aside the flexor sheath can be opened in the proximal and the distal direction. The adequacy of the release can be checked by lifting the tendon out of the wound. If there is a chance that the sheath will reform (especially if wrist extensors are weak and the ligament is thick), it can be resected.

2. Stabilization of the thumb interphalangeal joint (a temporary arthrodesis) in full extension or a few degrees of flexion by insertion through the thumb tip of a 2 mm Kirschner wire. The distal thumb joint should not be put in too much flexion as it will make it more difficult for the patient to open the grip passively by pushing it against an object (Fig. 14). Remember that usually no extensor is available. Sometimes it is difficult to obtain a Kirschner wire which is not too flexible and it may be necessary to use the smallest available Steinman pin. The wire should go almost to the base of the proximal phalanx but not into the joint and it is therefore advisable to make a mark on the wire with a cutter before it is inserted. The wire end should be driven beneath the cortex of the bone tip. It is wise to cut sharp wire ends before the insertion as this will keep down the number of wires coming out spontaneously later. Another way is to use a threaded wire instead of a Kirschner wire. However, I am not sure that this is the best way, as the very best grips seem to have been obtained in cases, where the wire has come out, was reinserted and after about two years the joint has ended up with ligament shortening, no pin and ten degrees passive flexion.

If, during surgery, the pin is inserted too deeply and is scraping into the metacarpophalangeal joint the best way to get it out again is to make a small window in the cortex of the proximal phalanx and from here push it out and shorten it.

The purpose of the temporary arthrodesis is, of course, to provide a broad area of contact between the index finger and the thumb pulp during the key grip.

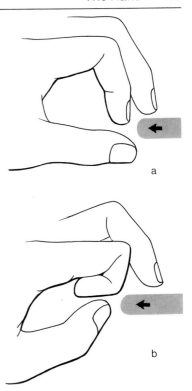

Fig. 14 The distal thumb joint should not be stabilized in flexion as this will make it difficult for the patient to open the grip passively by pushing it against the object to be held. a) correct, and b) wrong position of thumb in arthrodesis

3. Tenodesis of the flexor pollicis longus tendon to the volar surface of the radius.
This is performed through a curvilinear incision 6 to 7 cm long from the proximal wrist crease along the radial border of the forearm on the volar aspect. The palmar branch of the median nerve should be left intact if it functions. The flexor pollicis longus tendon is found on the ulnar side of the radial artery with concomitant veins, and it lies on the radial side of the flexor carpi radialis. It is freed from muscle fibers which are often attached to the tendon a long way distally and divided about 6 to 7 cm proximal to the wrist joint. Pronator quadratus is incised at the lateral border of the radius and elevated. The volar surface of the radius is now well exposed. To perform the tenodesis I make two windows in the cortex about 8 × 5 mm in size (Fig. 13) leaving a good cortical bridge between them. The spongy bone under the bridge is removed. The loose end of the flexor pollicis tendon is drawn through the most ulnar window and out through the radial window by means of a small wire loop.

The flexor pollicis longus tendon must *not* be taken out of the carpal tunnel (p. 62) and brought subcutaneously as this will impair the function. The tenodesis of the tendon must be made shorter than appears necessary as the bow stringing of the tendon will later leave some slack in the definitive reconstruction and other reasons too, make it necessary to start with a shorter tenodesis. When the thumb gets in position against the index finger, the wrist extension should not be more than about 15 to 20 degrees. As frequently in the same session other procedures have to be carried out in the same hand and arm, the last step to be completed will normally be the assessment of the length of flexor pollicis longus tendon in the tenodesis. Therefore, when the dissection is done, the windows are made and the tendon loop is in place, this incision is temporarily closed with a single skin suture and the rest of the surgery is completed. Then the incision is opened again, the loop fixed with a few sutures and the grip tested. The window technique has been chosen because it leaves the possibility of adjusting the tension of the tendon several times without added trauma. No drainage has ever been necessary.

The position of choice for the wrist in the plaster spica nearly always has to be a compromise between different "do's and don'ts", but must *not* put stress on the tenodesis. Often slight dorsiflexion is good and in such cases the thumb comes in under the fingers in the palm.

4. Dorsal tenodesis of the metacarpophalangeal joint of the thumb is often indicated when the passive flexion of this joint is so great that a broad surface key grip is not possible. In early cases it was often performed as a secondary procedure, but now the indications have become more obvious and it is usually included in the first step. It is usually to be recommended when passive flexion in the joint is above 30 degrees.

As no absolutely firm fixation is desirable, my technique aims to get a partly mobile fixation between the extensor apparatus and the metacarpal shaft. Through a dorsal midline incision, the bone of the metacarpal proximal to the joint is scraped free from periosteum for about 30 mm length and the tendons are made rough on the surface against the bone. At both sides of the tendon three to four pairs of small bur holes are made through bony cortex and one or two fine nonabsorbable sutures are used to encircle the tendons and the cortex beneath, bringing them into close contact (Fig. 13). Only one or two pairs of holes, as performed previously, will give too much mobility to the tendons and consequently too much joint flexion. If still more firm fixation is desirable, in some cases an arthrodesis with a K-wire has also been used, with or without the described tenodesis at the same time.

5. Transfer of the brachioradialis always means a change of the muscle from being a one-joint to a two joint muscle. Even more, it requires that the totally new function must be the most important. No doubt these are hard requirements!

But at the same time in patients with tetraplegia the brachioradialis is the forearm muscle most often available for transfer. It is frequently the subject for discussion. Repeatedly, it has been my experience that it is more difficult to reeducate this muscle to perform new functions than other transfers and the power of the final result often falls short of expectations. This, it seems, has not been mentioned in other reports, but in my own work an attempt has been made to extend the surgical help to higher levels of cord damage than before.

As experience was gained, I discovered that in cases with useful triceps function left there was stronger innervation of the muscle and better power after transfer. Conversely, when triceps was absent the action of the brachioradialis was very weak. The power could be increased by holding the forearm at the wrist to prevent elbow flexion (pp. 7, 89). A splint immobilizing the elbow had the same effect. In operations carried out by other surgeons, where this muscle was used to power flexor pollicis longus, I found that the power of the thumb was weak, but that this could be increased when elbow flexion was prevented.

To get a more accurate evaluation a measurement of the myoelectric activity in different situations was needed. As the EMG has a limited capability of producing quantitative information, I felt that the so called Biofeedback equipment would be of more use, and also easier to connect to the patients. After contact with the Med General, Inc. (Minneapolis) they gave me the opportunity to use their Biofeedback equipment during my recent stay at the Veterans Administration Hospital in Long Beach, where I also had access to a number of suitable patients operated on during my previous visit there.

One of them was a borderline case (American case 7, p. 89) without elbow extensors and in whom wrist extension too weak for function had been obtained by transferring the brachioradialis tendon to the extensor carpi radialis brevis. This wrist dorsiflexion could only be obtained when elbow flexion was prevented. When the myoelectric activity of the brachioradialis was assessed with the Biofeedback (Fig. 15) equipment testing active wrist dorsiflexion with the elbow free, only traces of activity could be seen and they faded quickly. However, when elbow flexion was prevented a much stronger response was obtained which lasted considerably longer. In the first situation only one or two red dots appeared for about five seconds and then they disappeared. In the second situation about ten dots appeared and they lasted at least 20 to 30 seconds. In another case with fair wrist extension, which definitely was of practical use, with elbow extension provided by a good deltoid transfer, the Biofeedback instrument showed a strong response on active wrist extension and this could be maintained for at least 30 seconds and could be

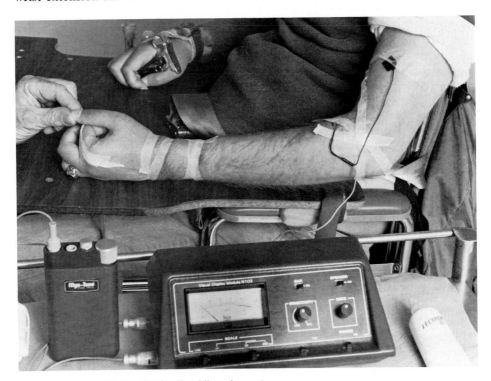

Fig. 15   Testing with the "Biofeedback" equipment

repeated. It was interesting, too, that when the instrument was used to assess the transferred part of the deltoid during wrist extension, it registered a strong response, thus showing the bracing effect of the muscle. A small number of these tests were all carried out with identical results.

These experiments show that the brachioradialis muscle, which in the normal arm is virtually only an elbow flexor, even if strong, does not readily perform other functions strongly when transferred. It is difficult to separate its function from the other elbow flexors, the biceps and brachialis. A prerequisite for good independent power in its new function is, therefore, the presence of an antagonist which can prevent elbow flexion, a stabilizer. The conclusion must be drawn that in cases where the brachioradialis is to be used as an active transfer, *the first stage of surgical reconstruction must be the provision of a substitute for triceps function, if this has been lost, i.e., a deltoid transfer.* If not, the result of brachioradialis transfer will be well below expectation.

The following transfers of brachioradialis have been tested in my work:

A. To the extensor carpi radialis brevis in order to obtain or reinforce wrist extension, the main acting force for most hands of tetraplegics. This transfer, therefore, is not required for the arms which already have strong wrist extension. For the others there are two different situations. Either the wrist extensors are very weak or absent, or together they have strength of about grade 3. In the first case one cannot expect contraction of the brevis to stretch out the adhesions that build up around its proximal segment as a result of the surgery, nor can the brachioradialis help if only an interlacing of the two tendons is performed. These adhesions will prevent gliding and also pervent the brachioradialis from dorsiflexing the wrist. Therefore, it is necessary to resect eight to ten centimeters of the brevis proximal to the junction of the tendons. If, however, the brevis is stronger, resection is not necessary and the brachioradialis is merely transferred. In both cases the junction is usually performed by interlacing one tendon into the other (Fig. 16a, b).

The rest of the operation is performed in the same way in all cases. The brachoradialis muscle is exposed through a long curved incision dorsally from the wrist up to close to the elbow. Skin incision should be planned so that its path will cross the line of the tendons at right angles rather than running parallel to them. The distal end of the tendon is freed and dissected proximally preserving the radial nerve and tying the small vessels to avoid hematomas, which could easily diminish the future functional amplitude of the muscle. An attempt should be made to achieve about five centimeters amplitude in the muscle before it is transferred to the extensor tendon. This means that the muscle must be freed almost all the way up to the elbow, to the level of the most distal innervating branches. If one stops the dissection just four to five centimeters before this level, only half the amplitude will be obtained which is not enough. Then the tendon part of the extensor carpi radialis brevis is freed from the surrounding fascia. With the elbow in about 40 degrees of flexion and with some tension in the muscle to be transferred, its tendon is threaded through small incisions in the extensor tendon in an interlacing way and anchored with small sutures (Fig. 16). This should be done proximally in the extensor tendon because more distally, less good gliding function will be obtained. Unnecessary length of the brachioradialis tendon is removed. This is perhaps the one procedure of all which requires the most careful technique to avoid scar formation, due to the very limited muscle resources to work with and the extensive dissection required. The follow-up work is nearly always hampered by the total lack of cutaneous afferents.

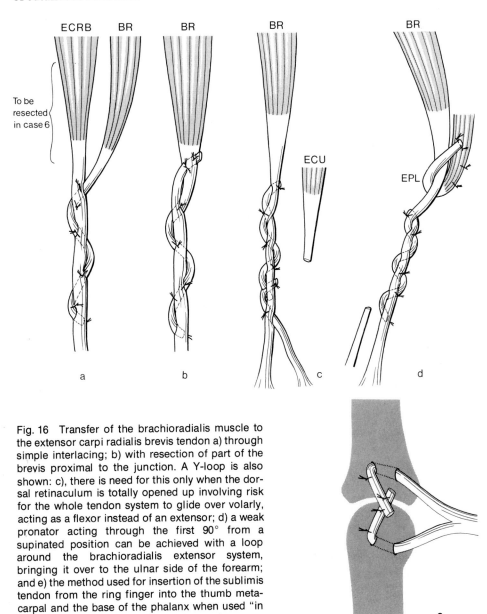

Fig. 16   Transfer of the brachioradialis muscle to the extensor carpi radialis brevis tendon a) through simple interlacing; b) with resection of part of the brevis proximal to the junction. A Y-loop is also shown: c), there is need for this only when the dorsal retinaculum is totally opened up involving risk for the whole tendon system to glide over volarly, acting as a flexor instead of an extensor; d) a weak pronator acting through the first 90° from a supinated position can be achieved with a loop around the brachioradialis extensor system, bringing it over to the ulnar side of the forearm; and e) the method used for insertion of the sublimis tendon from the ring finger into the thumb metacarpal and the base of the phalanx when used "in situ for adductor or "hanging-up" procedure

B. Transfers of the brachioradialis to the extensors of the fingers can be of great use as antagonist to the finger flexors in cases where sufficient muscle action is left to permit construction of active finger flexors. The surgery is in all principles the same as described above. Such a reconstruction, however, has to be a two-stage procedure, the extensor phase usually being performed first.

C. *Transfer of the brachioradialis* to the tendons of the flexor digitorum profundus is one of the ways to get finger flexion. In my series it has been tried out in very few cases only. The reason is that the number of motors for this transfer were rarely available and also that I have seen disturbing finger contractures resulting from this kind of surgery. However, now I have been convinced, especially by the cases operated on by Douglas Lamb in Edinburgh, that I have probably been too cautious to add this procedure to those which I have proved useful.

Other muscles for this purpose have been mentioned in the review of the literature, e.g., the pronator teres or the extensor carpi radialis longus. A warning is necessary here: never use the extensor carpi radialis longus if it is not *absolutely* certain that the brevis alone is strong enough for strong wrist extension. As is often the case, the effect of a transfer for finger flexion is almost as much a tenodesis as an active muscle function.

The brachioradialis is freed high up, as described before, and taken around the radius and interlaced into the profundus tendons and fixed with small sutures. Here, on the volar side of the forearm, it seems less important to perform a resection of the proximal parts of the paralyzed muscle-tendon unit to be activated than on the dorsal side. No doubt, the reason is the better supply of soft tissues on the volar aspect of the forearm with less risk of adhesions. The technique, in which the donor muscle is brought through a big window in the interosseous membrane, seems to be inferior to bringing it around the radius. The right tension in the musculotendinous system is very important. If as good thumb function as usual is to be expected, it is better to have the finger flexion a little weak than to get a disturbing contracture.

D. *Transfer of the brachioradialis* to the abductor or extensor pollicis longus or to the extensor pollicis brevis for thumb abduction. This procedure, which can only be done when the wrist extensors do not need reinforcement, is designed to provide active opening of the first web space for key grip. Although it is useful, the value of this abduction was less than anticipated since the patients seemed to compensate quite well for the absence of this function simply by pushing the hand against an object so that the space is opened passively (Fig. 14). It also took the patients quite a long time, sometimes over six months, to get accustomed to using the active abduction. Therefore, this transfer has often been postponed in order to keep the surgical procedure as simple as possible, especially when a patient's psychological condition made it desirable to minimize the extent of the surgery. Some female patients have objected to the long scar on the forearm. The decision of making the transfer to the abductor or to an extensor pollicis can be made only at surgery by making test pulls to the two exposed tendons. In one patient it will be the abductor tendon and in another the extensor, which ever one give the best excursions. The skin incision line should cross the tendon pathway at right angles as much as possible, to avoid adhesions between tendons and skin. An interlacing end to end junction with resection of the parts of the receptor unit proximally to the junction gives better gliding than without resection. The junction should be placed as far proximally as possible.

The transfer of the brachioradialis to the flexor pollicis longus tendon in order to get thumb flexion has, as described above, been used by several authors. However, all the thumbs operated on by this technique by different surgeons and later examined by myself have turned out to be inferior in power and gripping facility when compared to the tenodesis thumbs described here. Therefore for thumb flexion four brachioradialis transfers were used in my work.

6. Resection or division of the extensor retinaculum at the wrist. This permits bow-stringing of the active extensor carpi radialis tendon and increases the power of the wrist extensor. It will, of course, simultaneously reduce the amplitude of the motion obtained and can only be used when the muscle system has sufficient amplitude itself. The procedure involves a risk of subsequent radial subluxation of the active wrist extensor tendon, which can even make it a wrist flexor. This was seen in one case. To prevent this or to restore function when it has occurred, procedures 7 and 8 can be used.

7. Y-loop wrist extensor tendon (Fig. 16c). This is constructed by suturing the proximal end of the distal segment of the divided extensor carpi ulnaris tendon to the tendon of the active wrist extensor. The ulnaris tendon can be taken out of its tunnel. It must be left slack enough to ensure that when the muscle pulls, the wrist goes into both extension and into some radial abduction to increase power in the key grip. This is still able to prevent the radial subluxation of the extensor muscle system.

8. Loop retinaculum to the ulnar side of the forearm around the active extensor in order to achieve one or two aims:
A. A weak but useful pronator action when the pronator teres function is totally absent.
B. To counteract the previously mentioned radial volar subluxation of the active extensor system.
A sling is fashioned from the split extensor pollicis longus tendon or from the proximal part of this tendon (Fig. 16d) when it is nonfunctional. The thumb abductor can also be used. If nonfunctional, the tendon is transected one or two centimeters proximal to the wrist joint. The proximal segment is used to make a loop, which encircles the active wrist extensor system and is sutured to the firm fascial structures toward the ulnar side on the dorsum of the forearm in such a way that the blood supply of the tendon loop is preserved. For pronator action the extensor system must be brought all the way over to the ulnar side of the forearm on its dorsal aspect through the sling. This probably reduces its power for wrist extension slightly, and should, therefore, not be used in cases with very weak muscles.

9. Dorsal tenodesis of the extensor pollicis longus or the extensor pollicis brevis to the radius has been performed, usually as a secondary procedure. The purpose of these procedures has been to get abduction or extension of the thumb, when the tone in the paralyzed muscles was insufficient to open the interspace enough when the wrist flexed by gravity. It may also be necessary when the thumb carpometacarpal joint was so lax, that the thumb missed the side of the index finger in the key grip. As will be discussed later, (Chapter 10) it must be questioned how reliable some of these procedures will be in the long run. For the purpose mentioned last the procedure described below (13) is probably the better one.

10. Wrist arthrodesis may be useful in the very advanced contracture cases with a medulla lesion at high level, even though this is contrary to what is often taught. Such hands seem to be quite useless and the story is often heard that some years ago the patient could at least feed himself, but no longer can do so now (Fig. 2). A wrist fusion in very slight flexion can restore this lost function, together with the use of a strap around the hand for spoon and fork. Also, as will be discussed in the chapter on spasticity, this kind of complication can be reduced or eliminated by a wrist fusion. In addition, this operation improves the appearance of a hand in maximal flexion contracture. In my opinion, it is a great mistake to perform a wrist arthrodesis in order to get more muscles available for transfer to the thumb and the fingers. Very tragic cases of this kind have been seen. As only reversible surgical procedures should be used in tetraplegia if possible, a temporary arthrodesis with two or three totally buried two millimeter Kirschner wires can sometimes give the patient the possibility to test the result during a few weeks before the definitive surgery is performed. In my series, I now have a case where bilateral wrist arthrodesis was found to be useful. The arthrodesis can, of course, be performed with any of the many useful methods reported. Stabilization with Rush pin and staples after resection (Fig. 17) has the advantage that no plaster at all is needed, or only a

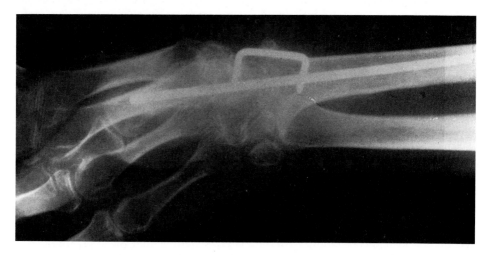

Fig. 17   Stabilization procedure used for wrist arthrodesis

dorsal spica for one or two weeks. Remember that considerable swelling occurs after this surgery and that therefore the dressing must be totally split, normally on the second day.

11. Denervation of spastic and irreversibly contracted muscles is a useful procedure and usually better than tenotomies, which often have a temporary effect only. Tenotomies, however, should not be totally discarded. Fairly often, spasticity and hard muscular contracture are localized to just a very few muscle units, more often than usually believed. It is very easy and well worthwhile to perform tests with a local anesthetic block containing adrenalin to try and localize the lesion. In one such case, it was possible to localize the spasticity by successively blocking the nerve supply to flexor carpi radialis, flexor carpi ulnaris, palmaris longus, flexor pollicis longus, and the flexor profundus to the little finger. The small nerve resections necessary were a very simple procedure and provided a great improvement for the patient.

12. Adductor construction, using the sublimis tendon to the fourth finger as a joining link between the active donor muscle and the thumb, is a good procedure in the infrequent cases where such a donor muscle is available. The total length of the sublimis tendon should be used and the tendon ends should, therefore, be detached at the insertion on the middle phalanx, the bridge between them divided and the tendon withdrawn through a small incision in the palm. From here it can be passed through a tunnel under the palmar aponeurosis to the dorsal side of the thumb metacarpophalangeal joint. The bone at the base of the phalanx is exposed through a curved incision and the tendon ends brought out. Two burr holes are made at a distance of about 7 to 8 mm apart and the tendon ends are brought in and out again crossing each other and fixed with a few sutures (Fig. 16e). The donor muscle is then joined to the proximal part of the sublimis system *in situ* in the forearm under appropriate tension.

13. A "lifting-up" construction for the thumb has been obtained in a similar way as the construction described for procedure 12. It is used as a secondary procedure where the thumb tissues have been so slack, probably by trauma from propelling the wheelchair, that the thumb hangs down too far and is unable to meet the index finger from the side. The only difference is that the sublimis tendon here must be brought out on the dorsal side of the hand through the interspace between meta-carpal II and III and that it must be anchored above the wrist to give a tenodesis, if the tone in the muscle is insufficient. When the wrist goes into extension the thumb is lifted up into the gripping position. This procedure has been tested only twice, as the situation is uncommon, but it has proved to be useful.

14. The Zancolli "lasso" operation (1974) is an ingenious way of checking dorsi-flexion (clawing) of the metacarpophalangeal joints of the fingers by use of the sublimis tendons or strips of them. This method could also be based on muscle tone alone if voluntary muscle action had been lost, i.e., even in cases with high lesions having clawing, where there is continuity between the muscle and the anterior horn cells (Fig. 18).

With kind permission of Dr. Zancolli, I quote the English summary of his original paper, published in Acta Ortopédica Latinoamericana and I also add parts of his Fig. 2 (here Fig. 18):

"Summary. The author describes a new operation which is indicated to correct the claw deformity due to intrinsic paralysis. It consists of the transfer of the flexor superficialis tendon, of the clawed digit, to lace (the "lasso" operation) the proxi-mal part of the digital fibrous sheath.

Correction of the claw is obtained through stabilization of the proximal phalanx during finger extension. During finger flexion it is possible to regain other intrinsic functions because of its action as prime flexor of the proximal phalanx: synchro-nous digital flexion; intrinsic plus position; stabilization and some increase of strength during pinching and grasping (Fig. 2).

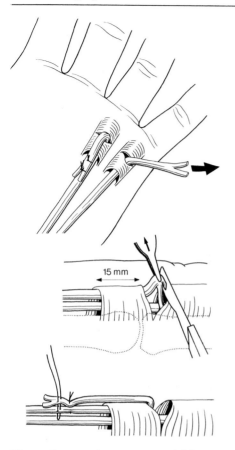

15 mm

Fig. 18 The Zancolli "lasso" operation. (After Zancolli, E. A.: Acta Ortopédica Latino-americana I: 1, 1974)

Up to date we have operated 13 cases with good results. Because of its simplicity and effectiveness to regain most of the lost intrinsic functions we recommend it as a very useful operation".

Having seen and tried his "lasso" technique it seems also to me superior to the other methods suggested for the purpose in question.

Order of Procedures

The order in which the different procedures are performed is important when several are combined in the same sitting. No case is identical with another and the planning must include the sequence of the procedures. The whole dissection on both volar and dorsal sides has to be performed before any suturing of transfers or fixation of tenodeses takes place. It is very difficult to judge the right length of the flexor pollicis longus tendon in its tenodesis to the radius before the distal thumb joint is stabilized. Therefore, it is usually best to start with the resection of the annular ligament around the thumb flexor tendon and the stabilization of the tumb joints, if these procedures are found to be necessary. These incisions can be closed immediately. It is always an advantage at the suturing of transfers to have as many as possible of the skin incisions closed in order to avoid later tension on the delicate junctions. The flexor pollicis longus tenodesis to the radius must be very exact and no undue tension may be applied to it once it is finished. The tendon is treaded through the windows in the radius and temporarily anchored with one or two sutures at an early stage. The definitive tenodesis is left until near the end of the operation. During the later stages of surgery, the operator must be sure that no unwanted tension is applied to already finished structures by the assistants handling and turning the arm as this might undo part of the work. He must also be aware of the risk, and if necessary counteract this risk, of local damage by muscle contraction during the extubation of the patient, while he is half asleep.

Elbow Extension

A functional elbow extension can be performed by transferring deltoid muscle function to the aponeurosis of the triceps. This procedure converts the transferred deltoid from a one-joint muscle to a two-joint muscle and apparently causes no functional loss at the shoulder that can be perceived by the patient. However, no quantitative measurements of shoulder function have been made before or after transfers. Unlike the procedures on the hands, which must be highly individualized, this procedure can be standardized. In the work previously performed, I have always started with a transfer of only the posterior part of the deltoid. Only in a few cases was the anterior part of the deltoid added later to the already matured extensor system in order to get more power. In my opinion, the deltoid is strong enough with the surgical technique described here to pull apart any attempt to join the whole muscle with free tendon grafts. At this point it is important to remember that a strong elbow extensor alone cannot elevate the body, not even from the sitting position. This function also requires sufficient power from the distal parts of the pectoral muscles, the trapezius and if possible some latissimus dorsi muscle. The latter is usually absent, in my experience it was present only in 20 % of all cases. Therefore, a moderate "triceps" function is often as useful as a stronger one. The partial transfer is based on the fact that the posterior part of the deltoid has an independent innervation. This part of the muscle is extended to the triceps aponeurosis with free tendon grafts from the toe extensor (Fig. 19).

Through a curved incision along the posterior border of the deltoid, the muscle is laid free along its posterior part as far as its insertion into the humerus. There is often a fibrous band of variable strength which goes from the deltoid to the brachialis muscle. This can be dissected free from the brachialis while still attached to the deltoid. If present, the fibrous band is helpful as an anchorage into which sutures can be placed. It is not too difficult to find a line of natural longitudinal cleavage of the two parts of the deltoid where the separation can be performed almost by blunt dissection. A pair of blunt scissors can be inserted under the posterior part of the muscle from behind and brought forward following the surface of the humerus. It can be brought out between the two parts of the deltoid and the opening widened. A finger can be inserted for further separation and the dissection close to the humerus extended proximally and distally, until the posterior part is totally detached from the bone. The muscle must be freed extensively in the proximal direction without damage to its innervation to obtain the necessary amplitude by passive traction of at least 30 mm. Only the aponeurosis at the borders of the upper parts of the muscle has to be separated by sharp dissection. The whole operation requires careful hemostasis. There are many bleeding points due to the number of circumflex vessels. If this is not done continuously, it is impossible to perform a proper dissection. The blood loss can be kept to an unimportant level. Only in one case was a transfusion used.

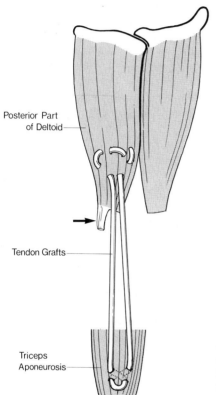

Posterior Part of Deltoid

Tendon Grafts

Triceps Aponeurosis

Fig. 19   Procedure to achieve active elbow extension. Posterior part of the deltoid is transferred to triceps aponeurosis (not olecranon), extending it with free toe tendon grafts. Arrow indicates fibrous band from deltoid to the brachialis. This is dissected out with the deltoid and is used to help secure the tendon grafts. (After Moberg, E.: J. Bone and J. Surg. 57 A: March 1957)

The procedure now continues with the exposure of the triceps aponeurosis which is performed through a curved incision of about 6 to 7 cm in length, some 4 to 5 cm proximal to the olecranon. The aponeurosis here is a broad band in the central part of which it is easy to get a good grip by interlacing a graft through a few incisions. Usually, I let the graft go back and forth through the aponeurosis twice and anchor it with a few stitches.

A good supply of tendon grafts is available in the form of toe extensors. They can be taken out through small incisions (Fig. 20). From the ankle upwards it is advantageous to use the Brand stripper. The tendons from the second to the fourth toe are the best. They are useless to the patient anyway, and there should be no hesitation to take enough. Many years after the accident they are still useful as grafts, but somewhat smaller and, therefore, three should be used. In other cases it may be enough to take two. This length of graft, from the base of the toes to about 6 cm above the level of the start of the muscle fibers is quite adequate to go from the deltoid to the triceps aponeurosis and back again with enough for the necessary interlacings. In the upper part the toe tendons join each other and should not be separated but used as an entity. The muscle fibers attached here are removed.

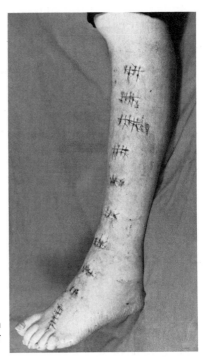

Fig. 20 Incisions for taking the toe tendons. With use of the Paul Brand stripper only the distal two or three incisions are needed

I start making a tunnel between the two incisions on the arm of adequate width going between the triceps fascia and the subcutaneous fat. The graft is passed from the distal incision up to the proximal one letting the joined part of the graft lead. This is interlaced a few times through the most fibrous part of the distal deltoid, and fixed with several small sutures both to the deltoid and also between the loops of the interlaced tendons. Some of the sutures will get a hold in the fibrous band already mentioned. The tendon graft is then passed through the triceps aponeurosis with the other divided end leading and is tightened sufficiently and fixed in the way already described. It is then brought up again to the deltoid through the same tunnel interlacing the deltoid again and then sutured in place. A few sutures may fix the down loop to the up loop. During the whole procedure the elbow must be kept straight (extended) and the arm abducted 30 to 40 degrees to get sufficient tension.

Often it is wise to insert a suction drain. The incisions are closed and a well-padded plaster spica is applied from the upper part of the humerus to just proximal to the wrist joint, keeping the elbow in about ten degrees of flexion. To prevent unexperienced attendants using the arm as a handle, a band from the wrist is attached to a band around the waist of the patient and left until the patient can protect himself. Six weeks of immobilization is required (Fig. 9b).

The strong deltoid can easily disrupt the newly formed tendon system when the patient comes out of anesthesia. This has not yet happened in my series, but I am aware of the risk from other similar procedures. Therefore, before the anesthesia has become less intensive, infiltrate the posterior deltoid muscle with a local anesthetic in order to paralyze it for a few hours. Twenty milliliters of xylocaine or carbocaine in one percent solution with adrenalin 1:200,000 is recommended.

After at least several months it is possible to transfer the rest of the deltoid to the existing extensor system in order to increase power. This is performed in a similar manner but without the tendon graft. It seems possible to shorten the immobilization necessary after the second operation by one or two weeks. This procedure has been used in four cases only, in three of them with success. In the other case it failed just as the first operation (case report 12, p. 89). The reason why it is not used more often is that the power obtained by the first operation was sufficient and the extra power was insufficient to make new activities possible. It did not improve the patients ability to transfer because of the lack of other adequate shoulder muscles.

Surgical Complications and Procedures Abandoned

Surgical complications have been relatively insignificant. The problems have arisen in the areas of judgment, surgical indications and the follow-up treatment.

No infection has occurred so far. Two hematomas developed under the proximal incision after deltoid transfer, but they did not influence the course of treatment. The only pressure sore to develop was on a digit where the treatment of the rubber-band traction was not sufficiently supervised, and it healed without any functional loss.

One patient died following an abdominal operation six months after he had regained a useful grip in the hand through operation.

Another case lost most of the function that had been gained in one hand due to increasing cervical cord compression.

Some of the Kirschner wires migrated spontaneously out of the thumb tip and the thumb assumed the Fromment's sign position when gripping was attempted. These patients had to be provided with a new K-wire after a few weeks. I have no record about how often this occurred but I think it could have happened in 20% to 25% of all cases. This resulted partly from the shape of the K-wires which were quite different in different centers, often too sharp. In very few cases this happened twice or even more in the same case. If this becomes a complication it can be avoided, as suggested by a colleague, by the use of threaded K-wires which seem to remain in place more reliably. However, I am not yet sure that this will be the definitive technique (p. 48). Besides, the procedure might not be reversible. It has never been necessary to perform bony arthrodesis in the interphalangeal joint of the thumb.

In some cases the dorsal tenodesis of the extensor pollicis longus (EPL) to the thumb metacarpal has stretched too much. It is very easy to adjust this and no doubt, with improved technique it could be avoided. Alternatively the dorsal tenodesis could be fixed with three or four sutures instead of the two which were used in some cases.

In three cases slackening of the flexor pollicis longus tenodesis to the radius occurred, usually caused by vigorous and too early propulsion of the wheelchair. It was quite easy to shorten the tendon distally in the thumb by another operation under local anesthesia. The tendon was anchored with a pull-out wire through the distal phalanx knitted around the nail. The thumb was then immobilized by a plaster spica for a further four weeks.

One procedure was tried out in two cases and failed and is, therefore, no longer used. This was the rerouting of the flexor pollicis longus tendon out of the carpal tunnel subcutaneously to the radius. The idea behind this was to get more rotation of the thumb. The result, however, was considerable loss of power in the two cases in which this procedure was performed. One case was revised with restoration of the tendon to the carpal tunnel. Improvement of gripping power resulted immediately. The second case, due to psychological reasons, was left with a grip weaker than ordinarily expected but it still had some value.

In some cases the extensor pollicis brevis tendon was used as an extensor tenodesis or, for those with extraordinarily good muscle resources, to supply opposition. The results were very poor. It may be difficult to evaluate these detailed results adequately in comparison with the more important functions under consideration obtained through the same operation. Further attempts to use this very thin tendon do not appear wortwhile. The only exception seems to be in its use for thumb abduction and extension with brachioradialis as the motor. In this function, unlike the others quoted, the tendon appears to gain strength. The brachioradialis muscle is slow to be retrained for new functions and it does not develop a very good control if triceps is absent. This may have some bearing on the better results achieved when it is used as a motor in just this situation.

Finally, in just a few cases some adjustment of the tension of a tenodesis or a Y-loop was required.

The number of these minor surgical adjustments and later improvements are of very little importance compared with the initial major problems which this surgery has to solve. With added experience there is no doubt that the need for such adjustments can be drastically reduced. If the problems with the interphalangeal pin are discounted the total number of secondary operations was 18 for the 105 hands and 40 elbows operated on.

9

Postoperative Reeducation

This is a very important part of the treatment and the final result depends greatly on the way it is carried out. It requires much more brain work than hand work. Performed with the right spirit and caution it can produce good results, even though the initial resources were very limited. Unfortunately, it is easy to destroy the final result in a very short time, especially the elbow extensor procedure. No "routine" physiotherapy program can be prescribed as the result will almost certainly be disastrous. *Every exercise must be active.* No passive tension produced by the human hand should be used, for the hand is far too crude an instrument. If tension on a structure is necessary the pull of a few grams is sufficient, but it must be sustained over a number of hours, another requirement which the human hand cannot fulfill. A variety of splints will be needed. Pain will inhibit the patients "going too far" and this must be respected. Instead of the pull by the human hand *small* rubber-bands can and should be used in many different applications as they are extremely useful (Fig. 21a–f). On the lighthearted side, I used to tell my collaborators in this field that it is of less interest if they are trained as P.T.s, O.T.s or C.T.s. They will not be perfect for this treatment before they are transformed into R.T.s – Rubber-band Therapists.

The Key Grip with Variations

The surgical procedure ends with the plaster splint as already described. In most cases this will be removed after three weeks and at the same time the dressing and the sutures will be removed. Earlier removal of the sutures seems to me not only useless but also dangerous. It is almost impossible to put on a new dressing and a new splint as accurately as the first, which was applied with the patient's muscles relaxed under anesthesia. Generally, when everything is removed after three weeks no more dressing is required. The arm and the hand can be washed with soap and water.

Fig. 21 Small tricks used during the early training. The problem that the index and middle ▶ fingers are not flexed enough to meet the thumb in a grip can be solved by a rubber band pull, (a) and (c) or by a tape (d); passive abduction is sometimes (b) achieved with a rubber or plastic tube splint (J. Bone and J. Surg. 38-A: 910, 1956); (e) later the patient is trained to "roll up the fingers" against the surface the object is placed upon; it is also shown how a rubber-band abductor can be applied; (f) shows how the wrist muscles are trained against a rubber-band pull, fixed to the wheelchair; (g) Rubber-band traction splint used to reduce contractures to the wrist and to the proximal interphalangeal joints without causing hyperextension laxity to the metacarpophalangeal joints (easily vulnerable due to lack of proprioception). American case 1

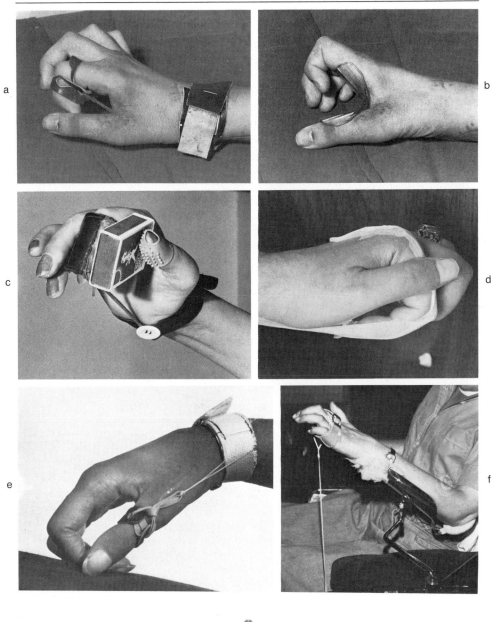

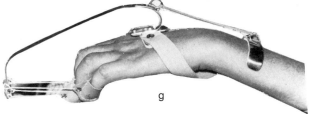

During the week following the patient is told to try and grip lightly with his hand and to wash it daily with white soap and water. The hand should never be soaked in warm water, this will only produce a dangerous edema which will organize to diffuse scar tissue. If the patient is able to raise both arms over his head he should do this many times a day to pump out the edema. He should avoid putting too much weight on the hand, but if he can bear some weight on the heel of the hand without straining the tendon involved in the surgery this can be permitted. If he is accustomed to pushing the pegs on the wheels of his armchair with the first interspace, between the thumb and index finger, this must be prohibited, preferably by supplying him with a chair without pegs. If not, this action performed during the first two months will easily cause slackening of the flexor pollicis longus tenodesis. During the first week out of plaster the key grip action should be demonstrated to the patient. He should not be trained yet but he should be acquainted with how the grip feels.

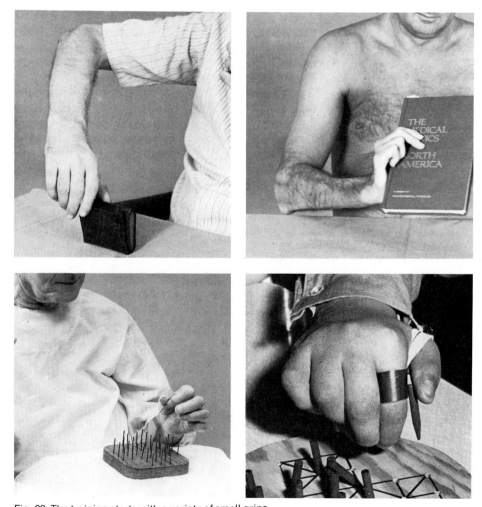

Fig. 22 The training starts with a variety of small grips

At the end of the fourth week after surgery active training can start, preferably with two sessions a day. Of course, the patient should have opportunities to practice the same grips on his own between the sessions. The aim of the occupational therapist (O. T.) is to provide him with a variety of activities in which he can utilize the key grip pinch, such as playing chess, handling pegs, picking up a small booklet, moving small wooden cubes, a matchbox, etc (Figs. 21 and 22).

No doubt the patient will encounter some regular difficulties when being trained. The most common are the following:

1. The thumb is too far into the palm and will not meet the side of the index finger. This is temporarily counteracted by the pull of one small rubber-band acting as a thumb abductor (Fig. 21e). With the thumb out just a little bit the oblique inner surface of the thumb pulp faces in the correct direction to approach the object (Fig. 14a). The problem that the index and middle fingers are not flexed enough to meet the thumb is also temporarily relieved by a pull with the rubber-band, or the index may be fixed with a tape (Fig. 21c). The proximal end of this rubber-band or tape is anchored to the wrist. Very soon the patient is taught to "roll up the fingers" against the table or whatever surface the object is placed on (Fig. 21e). Again and again one is confronted with the logical question "Why not overcome this difficulty with the help of a flexor tenodesis for these two fingers or even with an arthrodesis of the M.P. joints in slight flexion?" I have tried these procedures several times by making a temporary arthrodesis with K-wires and this improved the start of key grip training. But the patient's reaction has always been the same, "Please restore it to what it was before!" I have learnt from them and now I understand that these patients have an amazing ability to adapt themselves to the rolling up function. Perhaps in the future an extended use of the Zancolli "lasso" operation could side-step the difficulties mentioned without undesired side effects.

2. Passive abduction range of the thumb may not initially be sufficient even in maximum flexion of the wrist. This can be improved with a rubber-tube or plastic tube splint cut as shown in Fig. 21b. In combined action with the wrist extensors this splint will, of course, help increase the range of motion of the wrist which has stiffened to some extent during the necessary rest in plaster.

3. The temporary lack of mobility of the wrist must be treated. It is important to retrain the immobilized wrist muscles and commence new training of the transferred musculotendinous system which should be performed actively by means of another strap. This (Fig. 21f) can be fixed to the wheelchair and will permit almost isometric training of the brachioradialis and isotonic exercise with the radial wrist extensors. The forearm should be positioned in slight pronation. The skin is also improved as a result of this edema reducing pumping action.

4. Friction in these hands is reduced considerably in spite of the fact that the innervation of sudorimotor function may be retained. With the limited power available friction here is of paramount importance. The lack of friction is another of the many reasons why the three-pulp pinch should be avoided in tetraplegia, as the gripping areas are too small. Friction can be supplied by using bank note counters, carborundum tape on pens, forks and other utensils or by other means to make the surface rough (Fig. 23), either temporarily during training or permanently. This training and the accompanying encouragement soon enables the patient to continue by himself. He will be shown the different gripping possibilities (p. 70) and

will make a choice himself or perhaps find another new way to achieve the desired activities. A mutual search develops between the patient and the occupational therapist to look for ways to perform the activities of daily life. Every patient and every hand is different and apparently small details can greatly enhance function. Strength continues to improve over a period of years after surgery. When two months have passed after the removal of the plaster the risk of deterioration through slackening of the tenodesis is almost gone. It must be clearly understood that this is true only for the hand and not for the elbow extensor procedure. Again it must be stressed that it is almost impossible to train a patient adequately if, for some reason, he is bedridden. All that can be done under such circumstances is to prevent loss until he is able to get up again.

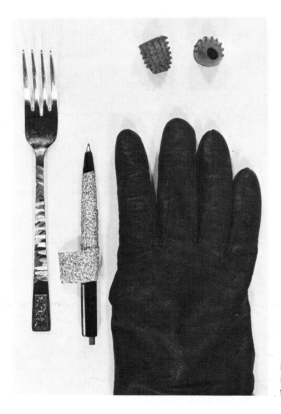

Fig. 23   Some means for adding friction, a most important part of hand function in tetraplegia

The Elbow Extensor Procedure

The main problem here is to get the patient and the occupational therapist to understand the fact that the free tendon grafts and their junctions to the deltoid and the triceps tendon must have sufficient time to mature and to be transformed into solid fibrous tissue which can withstand tension. For a very long time these structures must be regarded as if made of some kind of jelly which can easily be stretched but only with loss of the new function. The deltoid has only about 30 mm amplitude available and 30 mm is what is required to extend the elbow. Thus, there is not a single millimeter extra available.

This must be explained in detail to the patient as well as to the O.T., first before surgery and again when the plaster has been removed. It is my rule, based on experience, that if the O.T. has to go away for holidays or for some other reason she should not be replaced by someone else. It is better than to let the patient continue alone under the supervision of the surgeon. And of course, no stand-in doctors may be asked to help. A long and boring time awaits the patient when the plaster is removed. The desired power of extension is obviously there but it is of no use as flexion of the elbow is absent. Progress is so slow. It is almost an irresistible temptation for new occupational therapist taking over to please the patient by doing a little "better" than his usual O.T. How difficult it is *not* to increase flexion! This is the way the desired function is lost and all has been in vain.

While the arm is in the plaster splint it has lost most of the pumping action for fluid return and, of course, edema is likely to develop. In the arm itself this is counteracted by the circumferential dressing and the plaster shell. For the hand, however, it is often helpful to apply a compression dressing for about a week and after that to see that the patient frequently moves the wrist up and down. If necessary this motion can be supported by a rubber-band strap.

Usually, the patient can get up in his wheelchair after about two to three days. After a further two weeks have passed the only motions to avoid are shoulder extension and abduction more than 90 degrees. With the plaster splint in place he can very often propel his wheelchair himself. A patient with good facilities at home need not stay in hospital for very long.

After six weeks the plaster, the dressing, and the sutures are removed and the arm is washed with soap and water. It is astonishing to see that active extension at the elbow is possible at once, straightening from the 15 to 20 degrees of flexion of which the elbow is capable. The deltoid immediately knows how to perform the action it has never performed before. By elevating the arm and rotating it slightly, so that a little of the weight of the forearm is applied in the direction of flexion, it is also shown that the deltoid can extend against this little weight. Everyone is pleased, but now the difficulties start. The progress in taking up flexion must be very slow. As a guide I suggest that not more than 10 degrees a week should be added to the flexion, but this is not a fixed rule. It is very wise not to exceed this figure, but for some patients even that may be too much. Reeducation must be controlled all the time by making sure that full active extension against a very small amount of forearm weight is always possible. If this is not possible it is time to make a tough but necessary decision: further training has to stop and the arm is put back into the plaster in extension until active full extension is regained. This may take one or two weeks and so the course of postoperative therapy is prolonged. Immediate recognition of this loss of extension requires skill in the treatment. Nothing seems to be required to increase *elbow flexion* nor should it be attempted. It comes by itself and only *extension* has to be trained.

If possible, training should take place several times a day both with gravity completely eliminated and with gravity partially eliminated by abducting the arm to 90 degrees and internally rotating it slightly (forearm pronated).

Some more precautions are necessary. A cast like the original one is worn at night for about two weeks after removal of the first cast. A commercially produced ready-made children's knee splint can also be used (Fig. 9c). This protects the arm in case of dangerous movements during dreams or other lack of control, as the elbow flexors are strong and can do harm. During the day the arm can be free. The patient is permitted to use a wheelchair cautiously and he can raise himself on the extended elbow as soon as he likes as this is an isometric movement. About four months after surgery the patient can start rolling from prone to supine to prone starting on a hard surface, for example the floor. In quite a number of cases a patient who had completed postoperative treatment for one elbow with good results, has been left to manage the whole follow-up training quite successfully on his own when the second arm was operated on. It can be added that so far I have not seen a single case where full elbow flexion did not return, but again and again I have met cases where too much interest in obtaining early flexion had prolonged the course of therapy greatly and made the extension obtained weaker than it should have been. Finally, I have seen one case in which the extension the patient had on removal of the plaster completely disappeared during the training program (case 12).

10

Results

It is difficult to analyze the results in these patients objectively. As a rule the gains are relative and impossible to quantitate. For a normal able bodied person it is almost impossible to understand in detail the difficulties and problems the severely handicapped tetraplegic patient has to face in his different daily activities, both from psychological and physical points of view. To a great extent it is a matter of personal dignity, such as the ability to eat with normal cutlery instead of using special tools and appearing different from other persons.

Of course, the activities possible in daily life were assessed before and after surgery, but such differences cannot be summarized briefly or tabulated.

Most patients in the Scandinavian group have now had a sufficient follow-up time and their results can be given in full detail together with the time factors. As some of the patients are living close to Göteborg their progress has been followed more closely and their results will be discussed to a greater extent. This is in spite of the fact that they were the earliest cases operated on in the study when methods were in a more developmental stage. There was less experience and more mistakes were made. Some of their own impressions will be given in their own words.

For the American cases rather less extensive follow-up studies have been possible so far. However, an early but good study from Rancho Los Amigos Hospital is given. The results from the other patients must be summarized as they appeared when they were last seen. In some instances it is useful to give details where unexpected or astonishing functional features were present.

Gripping Patterns

First, as an introduction to the results, the gripping patterns should be discussed.

The main aim of my hand surgery in tetraplegia has basically been to obtain a "key" grip. However, in action it includes a variety of useful variations. It is often difficult to predict which of them will be the favorite one for a given hand or a patient. Variations in flexor muscle contractures in the four ulnar fingers, in ligamentous stability, and in sensibility are the important factors here, not small technical variations in surgery.

Besides the regular use of the key grip (Figs. 24a and d) it should also permit handling objects of moderate size, for example a drinking glass (Fig. 24b). For lighter objects contact is often made distally against the index finger (Fig. 24e).

The "interlacing" grip, stabilized with the thumb, has widespread use, for example in handling eating utensils (Fig. 24c).

The "ligament" grip, as I call it, holds the object between the index and the middle finger, both flexed at the metacarpophalangeal joints and stabilized sideways against each other by the taut collateral ligaments. Between these two fingers there are larger contact surfaces than in most other methods of gripping in tetraplegia and, therefore, more friction exists. The power comes from the thumb, adding pressure against the radial side of the index finger. It can be used for small as well as for larger objects (Fig. 24d). Another variation is the use of the thumb against the base of an almost fully extended index finger (Fig. 26).

A Brief Summary of Operative Results

Up to the end of February 1978, the total number of hand grip constructions was 114 on 97 patients. The number of elbow extensor constructions were 54 on 44 patients.
In Scandinavia (Sweden, Finland and partly Denmark), where the work was continued over years, these operations can be divided up in the following way:

Grip constructions on		Elbow extensor constructions on	*No. of patients*
both hands	and	both arms	6
both hands	and	one arm	3
both hands only			7
one hand only			19
one hand	and	one arm	10
one hand	and	both arms	3
		only both arms	1
		only one arm	2

This means 64 hands on 48 patients and 35 elbow extensors on 26 patients and altogether 98 operations on 51 patients. Some of these patients are still coming back requiring additional procedures where indications exist.
In the USA 51 hand grip constructions were performed on 45 patients and 17 elbow extensor constructions on 16 patients. Single operations, in 1978 as well, were performed in other countries such as Argentina, Great Britain, Spain, and Switzerland.
The first hand grip operation was performed in 1970 and the first elbow extensor construction in 1971.
A great number of these operations were performed by myself or with my assistance. Only two hand operations and one elbow extensor operation were performed by surgeons trained by myself but in my absence. However, I had seen these patients before and after surgery. Work continues on these and new patients at various locations (Fig. 25).
Operations on six hands and two elbows must be regarded as complete failures (see below). One of the latter, however, was reoperated with some success. These cases will be described in detail explaining what is believed to be the cause of the failure.
However, *no functional loss* occurred as a result of the surgery in my series so far. The only cost of the least fortunate results was the loss of time and the inconvenience caused. In some cases it is questionable whether the improvement gained

a

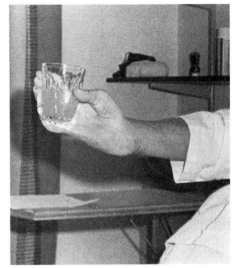

b

Fig. 24 a) The key grip (normal hand); b) the key grip used for holding a drinking glass; c) the "interlacing" grip in conjunction with the key grip provides stable clefts into which the fork is pressed; d) both hands operated on – the right hand shows the match in the "ligament" grip, reinforced by the thumb tenodesis, the left hand has the matchbox in a typical key grip (observe that the eyes must guide one hand; case 28); e) precision key grip used against the distal part of the index finger (case 10), guided exclusively by vision; f) playing chess before and

c

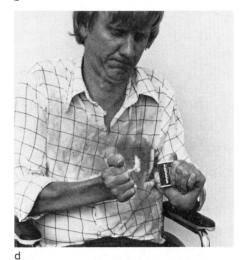

d

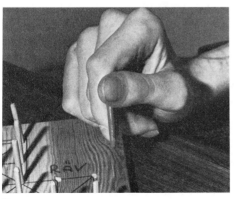

e

f

Fig. 24 g ▶

g) after surgery. The rubber tube splint used during training can be discarded later (case 5). (a to c and e to g reprinted, by permission, from Moberg, E.: J. Bone and J. Surg. 57 A: 2, 1975)

g

was worth the time loss or in some cases the extra burden put on the families. The rest were found to have made some useful functional gain, sometimes quite small, but sometimes quite substantial, as described below in more detail.

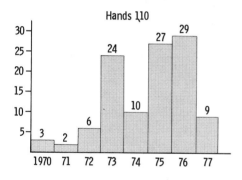

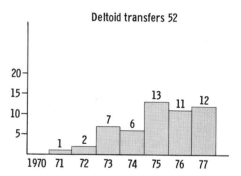

Fig. 25   Personal experience up to February 1978

Scandinavian Cases. Positive and Negative Results

Table 7, which is self-explanatory, provides the information.

Table 7. All Scandinavian cases up to end of February 1978

Case No.	Fracture or dis-location	Side hand operated on	Group	Side of deltoid transfer for elbow extension	Functions (right and left one-hand grip and elbow extension) restored	Remarks
1	C_3 on C_4	L	O:1			No improvement. See case report
2	C_5	L	O:1			No improvement See case report
3	C_5	R	O:1 O:1	L	2	Improvement
4	C_5	R	O:1 O:1	R	2	Improvement
5	C_5	L	O:1 O:0	L R	3	Improvement. See case report, Table 8 and Fig. 27 b
6	C_5	R	O:1		1	Took 6 months to obtain useful grip
7	C_5	L	O:1		1	Weak pronation obtained, made change to hand-driven wheelchair possible. Grip useful
8	C_6	R	O:1		1	Improvement
9	C_5	L	O:1		1	Grip was useful. Died following abdominal surgery
10	C_5	R L	O:1 O:0	R L	4	Special procedure on left side. Only for wheelchair. See Tab 8
11	C_5 on C_6	L	O:1			No improvement. Obtained a grip but never used it
12	C_5	R	O:2 O:2	L	1	Deltoid transfer failed. Grip useful
13	C_6	L R	O:2 O:1		2	Sensibility borderline. See case report and Table 8
14	C_5 on C_6	L R	O:2 O:2	L R	4	Sensibility borderline. See case report and Table 8
15	C_4 on C_5	R	OCu:0		1	Motor borderline. Improvement
16	C_5 on C_6	L	OCu:1 OCu:1	L R	3	Improvement. See Table 8
17	C_5	R	OCu:1 O:0	R	2	See case report and Table 8
18	C_6 and C_7	R	OCu:1 OCu:2	L	2	Improvement. See Table 8

Table 7 (continued)

Case No.	Fracture or dis-location	Side hand operated on	Group	Side of deltoid transfer for elbow extension	Functions (right and left one-hand grip and elbow extension restored)	Remarks
19	$C_3 - C_5$ $+ C_7$	R L	OCu : 1 OCu : 1	R L	4	See case report and Table 8
20	C_5	R L	OCu : 1 O : 0		2	Obtained grip, later deter-ioration due to spine com-pression
21	C_5 and C_6	R	OCu : 1		1	Improvement
22	C_6 on C_7	L	OCu : 1	L	2	Improvement
23	C_6	R L	OCu : 1 OCu : 2	R	3	See case report and Table 8
24	C_5 on C_6	L	OCu : 2		1	Improvement
25	C_6	R	OCu : 2		1	Improvement
26	C_7	R L	OCu : 2 OCu : 3		2	Improvement
27	C_7	R	OCu : 2		1	Improvement
28	No scelet-al lesion visible on x-ray	L R	OCu : 2 OCu : 2	R L	4	Improvement. Figs. 24 d and 28 a.
29	C_5	R	OCu : 2 OCu : 2	L	2	Improvement. Secondary procedure on elbow. See case report and Table 8
30	C_6 on C_7	R L	OCu : 2 OCu : 2		2	See case report with Figs. 26 a, b and Table 8
31	C_5 on C_6	R L	OCu : 2 OCu : 2	R	3	See case report, Table 8 and Fig. 27 b
32	C_6	R L	OCu : 2 OCu : 2	R	3	See case report, Table 8 and Fig. 24
33	T 1	R L	OCu : 3 OCu : 3		2	See case report and Table 8
34	C_5		OCu : 2	L	1	Improvement. Sceduled surgery to hand never per-formed
35	C_5 on C_6		O : 2 O : 1	L R	2	Does not want hand surgery because of paraesthesias; very satisfied with elbows. See Table 8
36	C_5	R	O : 1			Motor borderline. No improvement
37	C_5 on C_6	L	O : 1	L	2	Improvement. See Table 8
38	C_5	R L	OCu : 2 OCu : 2		2	Improvement

Table 7 (continued)

Case No.	Fracture or dis-location	Side hand operated on	Group	Side of deltoid transfer for elbow extension	Functions (right and left one-hand grip and elbow extension restored)	Remarks
39	C_7	R	OCu:4		1	Improvement
40	C_6 on C_7	R	OCu:2		1	Improvement
41	$C_5 + C_6$	L	O:1		1	Improvement
42	C_6	R	O:1 O:1	R L	3	Improvement
43	C_6 on C_7	R L	OCu:2 OCu:2	L	3	Improvement
44	C_7	R	OCu:3		1	Improvement
45	C_6 on C_7	R	O:1	R	4	Improvement
46	C_6 on C_7	L R	OCu:2 OCu:1	L R	2	Improvement
47	C_5 on C_6		O:0	L	1	Improvement
48	C_6	R	OCu:1 OCu:3	R	2	Improvement. Special indication to start with R
49	C_6	R	OCu:1	R	2	Improvement
50	C_6 and C_7	R L	OCu:3 OCu:2		2	Improvement
51	C_6		OCu:1	R	1	Too early for evaluation

Detailed Follow-up Studies of the Swedish Cases

The detailed follow-up studies of the Swedish cases were made during the last few months of 1975 and the beginning of 1976 by three occupational therapists (Lena Hermansson, Yvonne Dahl, and Barbro Wallander). Whenever possible the follow-up was performed by personal interview and examination. To this was added a questionnaire by mail. In a few cases this questionnaire was the only contact, sometimes reinforced by a telephone conversation. The follow-up study in twenty cases of twenty-six operated on is revealed in detail below. I would like to add that the results obtained in this way correspond with the results recorded by myself in these cases, either earlier or later, during personal interviews and examinations. I hold such meetings frequently, not only because the patients often spontaneously require further surgery, but also because I try to keep in contact with them as much as possible.

Table 8 gives the patients' answers written down by themselves in response to the questionnaire mentioned above. It is self-explanatory but a few comments may be added. First of all, it is easy to see how different patients evaluate the various activities gained as a result of an operation. This explains how difficult it is to predict what activities will be possible after operation and this is my own experience with the cases not included in the table. With further experience the ability to predict will improve, but even if functional gain can be foreseen, caution about detail is mandatory.

This applies to both positive and negative predictions. One patient was very keen to gain the ability to turn a round door knob. I told him that it was almost impossible to give him this special function. He was not able to let us observe the result after surgery but a few months later he was happy to let me know by telephone that he handled a door knob easily. I had been totally wrong. It can also be seen from the table that often a small plus difference in sensory as well as motor residual function after surgery not only makes more procedures possible but also more postsurgery activities.

At the end of the table are the cases in which, according to the results, no surgery should have been undertaken. Cases 1 and 11 would have been considered unsuitable today with the experience now available. There are several others where the sensory and motor resources were hardly more promising. Similar cases have often been anxious to have an operation although quite aware of the surgeon's doubt and have accepted what was obviously a gamble, although almost without risk of any loss. These are the very patients who have often had the mental spirit to make a gain from the small resources available. Why should such cases be denied a trial to gain the little improvement which can mean so much for one who has nothing or almost nothing left?

Detailed Personal Comments from Swedish Patients Given in Addition to the Answers to the Questionnaire

Case 5 (Fig. 27 a) I can wash my face and hair better. I need no help at meals. It is easier to hold a fork and spoon as well as a pen. I can manage keys with some difficulty. I have no difficulty opening drawers. I can now control the buttons on my radio and tape recorder. I want to have the other elbow operated on in spite of the fact that the hand on this side lacks the potential for surgical improvement. (This has now been performed and is appreciated.)

Case 13. Upper body hygiene is easier. It is easier to handle small objects and there is considerable improvement in opening drawers and in lifting down objects from above shoulder height. Perhaps my answers to your questions do not seem very positive. My feeling is that the surgery has made me much more independent in spite of the failure in the right hand. (This was a case where both hands were operated on in spite of afferent sensory function sufficient for only one.) My ability to get small objects from tables, shelves, and drawers is about three or four times as good as before. What this means to me can be understood by anyone with similar experience. (This patient is now employed as administrative aid.)

Case 14. Now both elbows and hands have been operated on and I have had training. I am able to dress and undress myself. I can manage housekeeping myself. It is easier to handle a drinking glass, eating utensils and a pen and keys. Transfer is easier, more effective and more certain. I can take down objects from above and replace them. I have got a driving licence which perhaps would have been possible without surgery but much more complicated alterations to the car would have been necessary. My hand power is very much increased.

The surgery has brought, and will bring about, more independence and less need for help. I do hope this surgery will be available for other patients in the future. I consider the improvement very valuable both from the physical and psychological point of view.

Case 17. It is no wonder I began to consider surgery for my arms. It is no fun to sit there with the orthoses on. I mean it is o. k. to be in a wheelchair, one looks normal, the only difference being that one is sitting all the time. But when the orthoses are fitted on a bit of the personal-

Table 8. Swedish patients. Answers to questionnaire: how has surgery altered the following skills?

Case No.		5	10	13	14	16	17	18	19
Group	R	(O:0)	O:1	O:1	O:2	(OCu:1)	OCu:1	OCu:1	OCu:1
	L	O:1	(O:0)	O:2	O:2	OCu:1	(O:0)	(OCu:2)	OCu:1
Activities									
Hygiene, grooming		+	+	+	0	+		+	+
Dressing		0		0	+	0		+	+
Meals		+	+	+	+	0		+	+
Housekeeping		0	+	0	+	+			+
Mobility Transfers		0	+	0	+	+	+		0
Handling pen		+	+	+	+	0		+	+
Handling keys		0		+	+	0	0	+	
Drawers Objects above		+	+	+	+	+	0	+	+
Buttons on TV etc.		0	+	0	+	0	+		+
Control of arms		+	+	0	+	+	+	+	+
Power		+	+	0	+	0	+	+	0
Years after 1st operation		3	3	5	4	3	4	3	3
Years after last operation		1	3	4	2	0	1	3	1

Group in brackets means that no surgery was performed on this hand.

Of the first twenty-six Swedish cases one died following abdominal surgery but had obtained a useful grip, one lost due to central deterioration most of the obtained function, five cases were at the time of the follow-up study too early to evaluate according to the table, but now have all useful function.

ity goes and one is made somewhat like a robot. So when I heard surgery was possible, I became interested. Of course, one tries to hide appliances from the eyes of other people as much as possible. Now when I want to do something by hand it is almost normal.

I can now wash the upper part of my body, hold the toothbrush and toothpaste and brush my hair. I can partly dress and undress. I can get some food and eat with a fork which has a thicker handle and added friction. I can write with a pen between the index and middle fingers adding power with the thumb and I can manage the radio and TV myself. I want the other elbow operated on too.

Case 19 (Fig. 28 d). The great value of this surgery is in providing more independence and this stimulates more activity. Without the right surroundings the gains are limited. In a jungle the tetraplegic is lost in spite of the surgery but in the right surroundings he can get a thousand things done.

I find grooming and washing the upper part of my body much easier. Previously I could not use deodorant or brush my hair. I am eating with regular cutlery and I can manage a glass. It is easier to control my wheelchair as well as open drawers and take down objects from above.

Case 23. After surgery I can use a knife and I can eat most food without assistance. It is easier to open drawers.

Case 29. It is easier to eat, to use a pen and to turn on the TV and use my wheelchair.

Case 30 (Fig. 26). I can now perform grooming and washing the upper part of my body.

23	29	30	31	32	33	35	37	1	2	11
(OCu:1) OCu:2	OCu:2 (OCu:2)	OCu:2 OCu:2	OCu:2 OCu:2	OCu:2 OCu:2	OCu:3 OCu:3	(O:1) (O:2)	(O:0) O:1	(O:1) O:1	(O:1) O:1	(O:1) O:1
		+	0	0	0	0	+	No result. See case report	No result. See case report	No result. See case report
			0	0	0	0				
+	+	+	+	+	+	+				
			+	+	+	0				
			+	+	+		+			
	+	+	+	+	+		+			
		+	+	+	+	+				
+		+	+	+	+	+	+			
	+	+	+	+	+	+				
		0	+	+	+	+	+			
		0	+	+	+	+	+			
4	3	3	3	6	4	4	2	4	5	2
–	2	3	2	5	2	3	0	–	–	–

Meals can be taken without special arrangement and with regular cutlery. I can do some baking and I can fold washed table linen. I can write without special equipment but the power is better with an appliance and I therefore normally use one. Small levers are fixed to my car keys so I have good control. Drawers at the right height present no problems. I am now able to mend things by sewing and I can do simple needlework. I have trained my grip this way – starting with a thicker needle and proceeding with smaller and smaller ones so that I now use a regular one. I am also able to thread the needle. (An example of her early needlework is shown in Fig. 26.)

Case 31 (Fig. 27b). The operation has improved my situation very much, not least in my job as I am soldering and using fine mechanical devices. My daily life at home has also improved. I can eat more easily as I can fetch the food myself and use a knife as well as a fork. I can handle pans for frying and cooking while preparing meals. It is easier to hold a pen and I am writing with one hand instead of two. I can use keys, open drawers and operate the switches on the radio and TV better and also take down objects from above and replace them. I have gained more confidence in controlling my arms and the power is much greater.

Case 33. Meal times are greatly improved and I can use ordinary glasses and handle open sandwiches. I can handle keys, drawers, take down objects from above, undo buttons and drive my car, which only required small technically modifications. The power of my arms has increased.

Case 35. My power is now greatly increased and I can transfer from bed to wheelchair and to car. Driving is saver and it is now easy to take down objects from above and replace them. (This was an exceptional case where in accordance with the patient's wishes only elbow extensors, on both arms, were constructed. This was probably a wise decision as marked paresthesiae were present in both thumbs.)

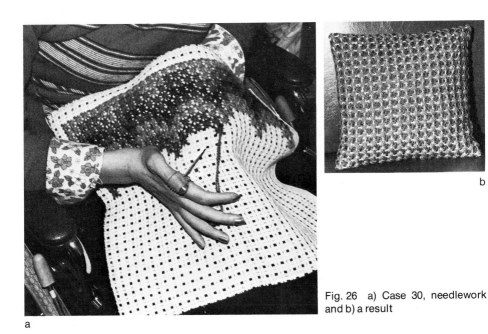

a

b

Fig. 26 a) Case 30, needlework and b) a result

A more Complete Follow-up Study of a Very Good Case with Surgery for both Hands and one Elbow Extensor

Case 32 (Fig. 28b). A 21-year-old man had a fracture of the sixth cervical vertebra resulting in tetraplegia. Both upper extremities were classed as OCu:2. The triceps on the left side was present with power 3 and on the right side had no function. In 1970 the right hand was given a key grip and thumb abduction and early in 1971 the same operation was performed on the left hand. Later in 1971 in the routine way an elbow extensor was constructed on the right arm. Before surgery he had tried to use hand driven orthoses but had abandoned them. In 1976 all function gained through surgery remained intact, instead power and facility had increased. The patient had moved from a service home for handicapped to a home of his own and had married. He was able to take care of himself while this wife was away at work. He could raise himself to a sitting position in bed, move unaided to the wheelchair from the bed (Fig. 28b) and from the wheelchair to his car (a regular car with special equipment for driving which was impossible before). He was right-handed just as he had been before the accident. The hand functions and their changes were recorded as follows:

Personal Hygiene

Combing: no difference, he uses a brush with attachments.
Washing upper part of the body: much easier, can now take down and hang up the towel.
Brushing teeth and shaving: he continues to use specially made attachements as before.
Use of handkerchief: much easier to get it out of the pocket.

Eating and Drinking

Use of spoon and fork: can use regular implements now and does so among friends. At home it is easier to use specially constructed implements.

Use of cup with large handle: function the same as before surgery.

Dressing: can now dress upper part of the body easier than before. He can get his shirt from a hanger above and can pull the shirt down more easily, can unbutton and pull the zip up and down more easily.

Miscellaneous Functions

Writing: can write with right hand and regular pen but still uses old pen attachment for letters as it is easier.

Use of typewriter: much improved; all the different controls and positioning the paper etc.

Tape recorder: can change tape and operate controls.

Handling letters in envelopes: much easier with new grips.

Handling newspapers and turning over book pages: much improved function.

Opening and closing drawer: no difference after surgery.

Turning water tap on and off: no difference after surgery.

Electric wall switch: no difference after surgery.

Use of keys: easier with new grip.

Handling matches: possible but not very certain.

Handling money: possible with new grip if the coins are on the table; cannot take bank notes from a pocket book.

Use of telephone: easier to handle receiver but uses pen for dialling the number.

Playing games: games with small sticks performed well with the new grips; can keep a limited number of cards in his hand, previously assistance was necessary.

Drawers: One of the great gains is the ability to take things out of a drawer. Previously he had to have things before him on the table and use both hands.

Housekeeping: he can now clear away china on a tray after a meal by himself instead of waiting for help as before. No function lost through surgery.

American Cases

It is, of course, far too early to report anything but some initial results from the cases operated on in the USA. However, in order to illustrate the endless variations this surgery offers, a few cases are reported here in some detail.

(1) A 49-year-old man with tetraplegia for 15 years was classified as O:1 on both sides but the left was better with wrist power of 3,5. The fingers on both hands had severe flexion contractures at the proximal interphalangeal joints and slight spasticity as the metacarpophalangeal joints were slightly hyperextended. The hands had an intrinsic minus position. It was obvious that it was not worth while operating in this situation. After several attempts a splint was constructed with rubber-band traction for the proximal interphalangeal joints giving simultaneous wrist extension but no hyperextension pull to the metacarpophalangeal joints. This splint (Fig. 21 g) succeeded after quite a time in bringing the fingers into an adequate position and surgery was performed to produce a simple key grip. A weak but useful grip was obtained. It might be possible to increase the value of the arm by adding elbow extensor function later, as he had no triceps function.

(2) A 45-year-old man with tetraplegia for 20 years was classified as O:0 on both arms and he had no triceps function. Five years ago this patient could use special equipment and splints to write, paint, feed himself and fire a gun (which he greatly enjoyed). Now severe contractures had developed at both wrists and in the fingers and he also had elbow and

shoulder contractures. He was now unable to perform any of the activities mentioned and even a two-hand grip was impossible. Resection arthrodeses of both wrists restored the two-hand grip and will make eating with a fork in a strip possible.

(3) A 41-year-old man who has been a tetraplegic for nine years was classified as OCu:3 on the right arm which also had a triceps with power 3.5. The left was classified as OCu:1 but with no useful triceps function. He was an active man doing accountancy with the help of a hand driven orthosis on the right hand, but he was unable to cut meat. His problem was that with the orthosis on he could not do the necessary push-ups for ischial skin care. It was too troublesome to take the orthosis off so his skin relief was often late and he got pressure sores repeatedly. A key grip was constructed with pinning of both distal thumb joints in order to get a grip, however, with the thumb gripping more distally than usual on the index finger. This grip made it possible for him to write better than with the orthosis, but still more important, it solved his problem of pressure sores. He was also able to cut meat with a regular knife in his new grip.

(4) A 65-year-old man who had been a tetraplegic for 12 years had an operation a few months prior to my arrival. An attempt was made to use extensor carpi radialis longus (ECRL) as a finger flexor and it was hoped that the extensor carpi radialis brevis (ECRB) was strong enough alone to dorsiflex the wrist. This was done on the left arm, which was the best side and classified as OCu:1 with functioning triceps. However, as so often happens, ECRB was too weak for wrist dorsiflexion and the wrist dropped. The patient was unable to feed himself and he lost all other hand functions.

Obviously, it was important to restore dorsiflexion at once. This was achieved through a release of the ECRL with transfer of this tendon as well as brachioradialis to ECRB. The distal thumb joint was stabilized and this improved his restored function (Fig. 22 d). A similar case was described by Michaelis (1964) in his book.

(5) A 37-year-old man who had been a tetraplegic for five years was classified as OCu:1 on the right side with triceps power 2.5 and OCu:7 on the left arm with a good triceps. The right hand had no single hand grip but his left hand grip was fairly good except that the thumb was very weak due to absent thenar function. His greatest difficulty was due to the lack of thumb adduction. Before his accident he was right-handed but now he wrote with difficulty with the left hand. It was suggested to the patient that he should have key grip surgery for his right hand initially as it was almost useless. He did not accept this advice, deciding that what could be offered to improve his right hand was insufficient. He requested that an adductor pollicis should be constructed and this was done by transferring ECRL, elongated with a palmaris longus graft, through the second metacarpal interspace to the adductor tendon and hood. At the same time an attempt was made to achieve opponens function by transferring flexor carpi ulnaris to the rerouted extensor pollicis brevis through the canal of Guyon. This failed as did most operations using the extensor pollicis brevis tendon, which seems to me too thin for most purposes. No opposition was obtained but he gained a very strong adductor. When he saw the result the patient also asked for the key grip procedure for the right hand. This was done by transferring brachioradialis to ECRB and performing the rest of the technique in the usual way. The result was that the left hand improved sufficiently to let him use a hammer. The right hand procedure, in spite of the patients pessimism, gave him a good second hand with a fairly strong grip. To have two functioning hands was completely new to him and he commented that these operations made him "change from a quad to a para". Of course, this was an exaggeration, but it was a sign of how rewarding this surgery can be for the surgeon as well as for the patient.

Follow-up Studies at Rancho Los Amigos Hospital

In a paper, given to the staff at the Rancho Los Amigos Hospital in November, 1976, Mr. J. H. Newman, F.R.C.S., has reported the results of a follow-up study performed by him on the cases operated on during 1975 and 1976 at this hospital. He performed a few of the operations himself, and has kindly permitted me to include in this book the part of his report cited below.

Results

Between October, 1975, and June, 1976, 24 key grip procedures were performed at Rancho Los Amigos Hospital. These cases have recently been reviewed and although the follow-up is short (four months to one year), it is possible to gain an impression of how much benefit the patients are deriving from this form of reconstruction.

The number of complications has been relatively small. One postoperative death occurred, probably due to delirium tremens following alcohol withdrawal. Of the remaining 23 patients, six have had problems with migration or misplacement of the pin in the thumb, but since changing to a threaded pin, no further troubles of this nature have been encountered. Three patients have had slight problems from stretching of the extensor pollicis longus tenodesis, and in one patient the flexor pollicis longus tenodesis required tightening. Most patients mention that some loosening of the flexor pollicis longus tenodesis occurs in the first few weeks, but provided the initial tension is correct, this does not impair function.

Overall, 20 of the 23 remaining patients have expressed satisfaction with the outcome and the reasons for the three failures are easily seen and could now be prevented. Eighteen patients have managed to discard their wrist driven flexor hinge splints, and are able to write and eat unaided. Some mention that prolonged writing can cause fatigue though patients with strong wrist extension can generate a side pinch of up to 18 lb/sq. in., which provides a very satisfactory grip for many purposes. Several patients have mentioned that in addition to discarding their splints they have been able to increase their range of activities following surgery. For example, one man can now do simple cooking and a lady is able to paint. A few patients find the grip of benefit in dressing.

In all the satisfactory cases the hand has remained supple and the procedure has not interfered with transferring between bed and chair, or with propelling a wheelchair. It is sometimes necessary to adjust the technique the patient uses for these activities so as not to damage the tenodesis with these vigorous maneuvres, but this has never been a problem.

Results of the Elbow Extensor Construction

Even if the results of elbow extensor construction in general are more uniform (Fig. 27 and 28) and so easier to judge than the hand work, interesting observations are possible. Generally, the elbow extensor power after surgery is several times stronger with the arm at the side in the position for lifting the body than with the limb extended overhead. The lifting power also depends on the function of the muscles fixing and bringing down the shoulder girdle. In paraplegics these are mainly the distal part of the trapezius, latissimus dorsi, in the few cases where it is present, and the costal part of the pectoral muscles which are more commonly functioning. A few tetraplegics get up into the sitting position without an elbow extensor by locking the elbows in hyperextension but this frequently involves the risk of falling forwards. The power of the elbow extensors and the shoulder fixing muscles required by a tetraplegic patient to slide on a board from the bed to a wheelchair or from a wheelchair to a car without help is much smaller than is realized. A downwards and sidewards force of 6 to 7 kg is certainly sufficient to provide a momentary thrust in each arm of up to 15 kg. One Scandinavian patient (case 35) who did not want hand surgery had deltoid transfers on both sides and could support 3 or 4 kg with each of his elevated arms. He was pleased to report that he could get in and out of his ordinary car on the board without any help. His pectoral muscles were evaluated as power 4 for the clavicular part and 0 for the

a   b

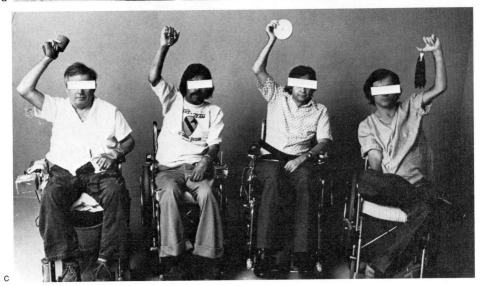

c

Fig. 27   Elbow control and extension restored through a deltoid transfer. a) and b) case 5 and 31, and c) four American cases

costal part on each side. Latissimus dorsi was power 2 on one side and 1 on the other side. This is not the usual result but it has been achieved in a few cases.

As we surgeons normally see the patients in their wheelchairs, it is easy to forget how many hours they spend in bed not only when medical complications require treatment. Almost everyone of the patients was asked about their views on the importance of the elbow functions in bed. It is less often commented on spontaneously, probably because they assume it is obvious to us. The patients confirm that the control of stability of the elbow means a lot even in bed. Some say that when smoking it is not only a nuisance but also a risk, because the arm, holding a lighted cigarette, uncontrollably comes down on to the face or the bed. "My range of motion has increased so much" is another point of view (Fig. 28c) which is often heard. Another is the general feeling of security generated by having stronger arms and the improved driving possibilities. The record for power after transfer is held by a strong Finnish patient (case 28) who can lift 7 kg straight up from the sitting position. Probably the best recommendation in favor of this procedure is that the patients so often return for operation on the second arm even if single hand grip is not possible for the second side.

Of the 38 elbow procedures performed so far only one was a total failure. One failed initially but the tendon was later shortened and the result looked promising. Subsequently, part of it was lost again. Now two years later he can fully extend the elbow against the weight of the arm but only until the proximal part of the arm in sitting position is elevated 60 degrees above the horizontal level. He lived a long way away from me and it was not possible to supervise his training personally. Despite the clear advise I had given him, local doctors and physiotherapists on both occasions said there was no risk in advancing quickly with flexor training and

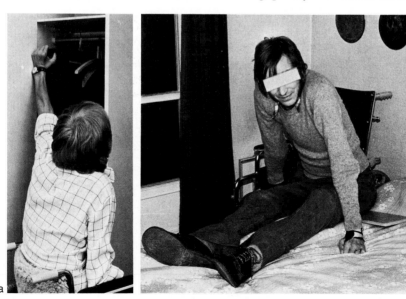

Fig. 28   a) "I can take down objects from above and replace them" – case 28; b) "I can raise myself to a sitting position in bed, move unaided to a wheelchair from bed and from the wheelchair to the car" – case 32.

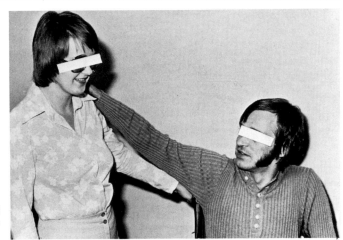

Fig. 28 c) the patient said: "My range has increased so much".

Fig. 28 d) case 19, both hands and both elbows operated on.

so he was given the elongation of the tendon grafts described above. He would like to have a second shortening of the good tendon and this should give him better extension (see the chapter on follow-up treatment). A few other cases are rather weak in extension and can just manage the weight of the arm but they still feel that this surgery has been very useful.

An interesting observation is that the brachioradialis muscle works better as a transfer, for example to the extensor carpi radialis brevis or to the abductor pollicis longus if it has a muscle antagonist in form of a transferred deltoid (p. 51).

Pinch Tests After Surgery

During training after surgery a few tests were made in order to evaluate the power of the grip. These tests (Table 9) were performed on the cases operated on at the Veterans Administration Hospital in Long Beach and by the occupational therapist Evelyn Mac Clean whom I have to thank for the results of most of these tests.

An American pinch meter from B & L Engineering was used, the results are therefore given in pounds. No measurable power existed in the pinch before surgery.

Table 9. Results of pinch tests on hands operated on. Pinch in pounds inch^2

Group	Key grip with brachioradialis transferred to extensor carpi radialis brevis = + Key grip moved only by carpal extensors = −	Weeks after removal of plaster:				
		1	2	3–4	6–5	More than 6 weeks
0:1	+			3		
0:1	−			$4^1/_2$		
OCu:1	+	2				
OCu:1	+ ∙	2				
OCu:1	+			$1^1/_2$		
OCu:1	+		$1^1/_2$		2	
OCu:2	−	4				
OCu:2	−	$2^1/_2$	3			4
OCu:2	−	4		8		
OCu:2	−			3		
	Other Grip constructions					
OCu:4	Brachioradialis transferred to flexor digitorum profundus and extensor carpi radialis longus to flexor pollicis longus	4		7	11	
OCu:5	Brachioradialis transferred to flexor digitorum profundus and extensor carpi radialis longus to flexor pollicis longus		3	4		
OCu:7	Extensor carpi radialis longus transferred to adductor pollicis		3	4		

In nine cases the key grip gave the following results, measured about one year after surgery: 9, 8, 9, 8, 8, 16, 2, 6, and 8.

Great care should be taken in the use of these tests because soon after the removal of the plaster tendons can rupture and stretching of grafts and tendon sutures can not be excluded. None have been observed to give way due to the test, but this risk explains why so few tests have been done. Early slackening has been observed under other conditions, for example by straining the grip in wheelchair propulsion or by attempts to widen the grasp for holding a drinking glass before adequate healing or before fibrous tissue has adequately matured (Chapter 10). I have doubts, therefore, about the need to introduce pinch tests as a routine in follow-up treatment.

Table 9 shows a great variation between individual cases and also how pinch power increases after removal of the cast as the weeks pass. Another interesting fact is that the key grip in hands with severe deficit can give similar or more power than adductor/flexor construction in a hand with better initial function. The pinch power should never be regarded as a measurement of the usefulness of the hand, many varied and more important considerations are involved.

Cases Operated on but not Improved

A small number of cases gained nothing from operation. However, they lost no function. They will be considered in several groups: firstly, the hand cases where gain was expected and secondly, the hand cases where there were minimal resources but both patient and surgeon judged it to be worthwhile to attempt surgical improvement. The third group are the elbow extensor cases. As only about a third of the American cases could be followed up so far no doubt a few more cases will be found amongst them. A loss, however, should have been registered.

Hands – Improvement Expected but not Achieved

Case 1 (Table 7). A 36-year-old man had a dislocation of the third cervical vertebra resulting in tetraplegia. Both upper extremities which were classed O:1, Tr 0, had no useful hand sensation and only a grade 4 brachioradialis associated with much flexor spasticity. Before operation he did not have one hand grip and could not use a hand-operated wheelchair. His left hand was dominant. Fourteen months after the accident procedures 1, 2, 3, 5A, 8 and 11 were carried out on the left. The transfer was never strong enough to overcome the flexor spasticity and no grip was obtained. The mistake here was to misinterpret the degree of imbalance between available active muscle power and the spasticity. Besides, the start should have been made with a deltoid transfer.

Case 2 (Table 7). A 22-year-old man had a fracture of the fifth cervical vertebra resulting in tetraplegia. Both upper extremities were classified O:1, Tr 0, the right dominant side having a grade 4 brachioradialis and a grade 3.5 radial extensor. On the left side the brachioradialis was grade 4.5 and the radial extensors were grade 2. There was some spasticity bilaterally. Four and a half years after the accident procedures 1, 2, 3, 5A and 7 were performed on the left. When surgical treatment was planned with this patient, who came early in the series, I was not yet aware of the fact that with only visual afferent pathways only one hand can be used for independent grip. Cutaneous afferent impulses were of low quality in both hands with no twopoint discrimination. The nondominant hand was chosen to lessen the risk of loss of function. The patient gained the ability to lift a pocket book and small objects with his key grip but never used this ability, preferring to use his dominant hand in supination and a two-hand grip to pick up objects as he had done preoperatively. The mistake here was to operate on the nondominant hand in the absence of sufficient sensibility.

Case 13 (Table 7). Already described among the personal comments from the Scandinavian cases. Both hands were operated on, but afferent impulses were only ocular and so one hand was useful, the other in spite of gripping motor facilities was never used and the patient, of course, found the surgery to be a failure. An early case.

Case 11 (Table 7). A 52-year-old woman had a fracture of the sixth cervical vertebra resulting in tetraplegia. The right upper extremity was classified O:0, Tr 0 and the left O:1, Tr 0. The left brachioradialis was grade 4 and the wrist extensors grade 3, and she had no hand function at all. Two years after the accident, procedures 1, 2, 3 and 5A were carried out on the left. However, the patient was unable to cooperate and postoperative training was impossible. The patient could grip small objects placed in the open first interspace but she never used the grip independently and continued to ask for help with everything. The mistake was to operate on a patient lacking motivation to cooperate. Closer study of the patient before surgery would have made this apparent.

American case 6. A 47-year-old man who had been a tetraplegic for 18 years was classified as OCu:3 on the right arm and OCu:3 on the left. Both sides had useful triceps muscles. Both hands were in extreme intrinsic minus positions due to fixed contractures mostly in the superficialis muscles but some in the joints, especially in the middle finger of the right hand. When studying his daily activities, it was found that he had to do the shopping for himself. When observed in his van it was obvious that the contracture was essential for driving. On the leading hand a key grip operation was performed, but due to extremely slack joint ligaments to the thumb it turned out to be too weak. The patient's comment was: "No gain, no loss."

Hands – Surgical Improvement Attempted Despite Only Minimal Resources

American case 7. A 22-year-old man had a fracture of the fifth cervical vertebra resulting in tetraplegia. The right upper extremity was classified O:1, Tr 0, although brachioradialis was only 3.5 and the wrist extensors were 0. Probably the arm should have been classified O:0, which was the rating given to the left arm. One year and nine months after the accident procedures 1, 2, 3, 4, 5 A, 6 and 8 were carried out on the right arm. This very cooperative patient has not yet achieved any useful active wrist extension and, therefore, a year after surgery has no grip. He was one of the patients who demonstrated the necessity of an antagonist (Fig. 15). No doubt it was a mistake not to give him an elbow extensor before the hand surgery. The Scandinavian case 36 is a very similar one (Table 7).

American case 8. A 25-year-old man had a fracture of the fourth cervical vertebra resulting in tetraplegia. He normally used his right hand with splints although his left hand was more powerful. The right arm was classified O:0, Tr 0 and the left O:1, Tr 0 as he had a grade 4 brachioradialis, wrist extensors grade 0 but a grade 2 pronator teres. Eight years after the accident procedures 1, 2, 3, and 5 A were carried out on the left but in the first six months after surgery he has not developed any wrist extension strong enough for a grip. However, in one similar case classified O:1, Tr 0, with brachioradialis grade 4 and wrist extensors grade 2 it took six months to gain active wrist extension and still longer to develop a small but useful grip. Although no gains have been made in these cases it is still possible that improvement will occur but by now it is unlikely if an elbow extensor is not added.

Elbow Extensors

Case 12 (Table 7). A 28-year-old man had a fracture of the fifth cervical vertebra resulting in tetraplegia. No triceps function remained on either side. Fourteen years after the accident the posterior part of one deltoid muscle was transferred to the triceps tendon using free grafted tendons from the toe extensors. When the plaster cast was taken off he was able to extend the elbow but this power soon disappeared. Later on an attempt was made to transfer the rest of the deltoid of this arm to the long tendon system which had been made. The result was the same. His follow-up treatment could not be supervised closely and it is my firm belief that this impatient man increased elbow flexion too quickly and the result was a disaster.

Case 29 (Table 7). A 36-years-old man had a fracture of the fifth cervical vertebra resulting in tetraplegia. No triceps remained on either side. Two years after the accident a routine posterior deltoid transfer to triceps was performed using free toe tendon grafts. When the plaster cast was taken off he had elbow extension. However, when elbow flexion had been restored the active extension control was almost lost and only very weak movement remained. Yet, the tendon and the muscle were clearly palpable. Therefore, nine months after the first operation the tendon was shortened. When the plaster cast was taken off he had good extension again but this was partly lost a second time. This patient, too, belonged to those who were seen occasionally on visits to another city and whose follow-up treatment had to be left to the local staff, who had been carefully instructed. This was several years ago and the patient now has power to control the arm in bed and can just extend the elbow against the weight of the arm until shoulder elevation is 60 degrees above the horizontal. He cannot get his arm any higher without losing elbow control.

He tells me that elbow flexion was, even this time, allowed to proceed much faster than recommended. The local staff had told him that there would be no danger to the power of extension. The result is not what he or the surgeon expected, but there is still an important improvement.

11

Upper Limb Contractures

Contrary to the great interest shown in many books and papers in the prevention of contractures during the acute stages of treatment in tetraplegia and during the first year, this problem is rarely discussed concerning the ensuing decades of the patient's life. One almost gets the feeling that the risk of deterioration is supposed to have disappeared. But this is certainly not so at all. My experience from centers where patients are coming in again and again has shown how dreadfully real this creeping risk continues to be for the rest of the patient's life, and how often very late hand and arm functions as well as independence will be lost. This ist not surprising. The harmful forces will continue to work twenty-four hours a day. Lack of proprioception, muscular imbalance, tone in muscles in connection with anterior horn cells but without central control, the weight of the arm, all of these are contributing to contracture.

No fight against pressure sores or urinary and bowel complications can be fought succesfully without the cooperation of the patient. It is the same with contractures. It must be clearly understood and accepted that ranging once or twice a day is *not* sufficient to counteract the factors causing contractures. A time will come when it will be natural to teach every patient what to do to avoid this deterioration as well as the other complications mentioned.

In order to help with this a small pamphlet was produced at the Veterans Administration Hospital in Long Beach and is with due permission reproduced here.

In late and difficult cases surgical procedures can give a little help. It is possible to denervate muscles with just tone or with spasticity. Tenotomies are less helpful as the contracture easily develops again. For the elbow contractures the brachialis muscle is the most important one and can be resected without functional loss. In all surgical cases the treatment must be combined with long time rubber-band traction (cave pressure sores) prior to and following surgery. Only in cases where it is felt that the patient has sufficient will and endurance to cooperate is a surgical trial worthwhile.

Some experience with similar treatment for the upper limb has already been gathered, but it is far too early to give details. The situation is markedly different from the one for the lower limb, for which extensive literature exists (Michaelis 1964).

The Upper Limb of the Tetraplegic

A Brief Manual for the Patient. Protection of the Shoulder, Elbow and Hand Joints

Before you became tetraplegic you probably took your arms, hands and fingers for granted. It is only when a person *looses* normal feeling and the use of his arms that he realizes how important they are. In fact, only *you* know how valuable your arms, hands and fingers are to you.

Now that you are tetraplegic, it is particularly important that you increase the functions of your arms, hands and fingers to a maximum and prevent them from deteriorating any further. Your therapists can *help* accomplish this, but ultimately it is *your* own responsibility.

The main purpose of this paper is to teach you what *you* can do for yourself to help increase the function of your arms and hands and prevent further deterioration. With proper exercise you can prevent the inevitable risk of slow, progressive muscle and joint deterioration in this part of your body. First, however let us discuss how deterioration occurs and where it occurs.

The Shoulder

While in bed or in a wheelchair, your arms are seldom lifted over head and instead they tend to lie in a dependent position beside your body during most of the day. This gives these unused muscles and joints a chance to shorten and contract from disuse. After a certain progress, these contractures become irreversible. Not only do they greatly reduce the range of motion of the joint, but they can also cause pain. The reason for these phenomena are poorly understood but they are an unpleasant reality.

The Elbow

In most tetraplegics, the muscle which extends the arm at the elbow (triceps) is weak or paralyzed. Since the muscles which flex the arm at the elbow (biceps, brachioradialis, etc) are often stronger than the elbow extensors, the flexor muscles overcome the action of the extensors. This can potentially result in a flexion contracture which limits one's range of motion. If this becomes irreversible, surgical repair becomes impossible and one is never able to fully extend the arm. Obviously, it is essential that everything be done to prevent contractures from reaching this irreversible stage.

The Wrist and Hand

The worst of all the contractures are those of the wrist and hand. As can be seen in Fig. a, the hand becomes permanently bent (flexed) at the wrist. The story is often heard: "five years ago I could feed myself, but now ..." And yet this, like the pressure sores, can be prevented.

These contractures develop partly because even a totally paralyzed muscle retains "tone" and is sufficient to pull like a rubber band, on a sustained basis. Another factor is the weight of the hand which, while in bed, tends to bend the wrist in the

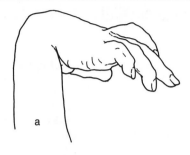

a

flexed position. But most important, however, is the fact that the hand has lost sensation so that you cannot tell its position and motion unless you look at it.

Prevention

What can be done to prevent these contractures?

First of all, keep the possibility of their occurrence in mind so that when you notice them in their early stages you can call it to the attention of your physician or therapist while it can still be counteracted, prevented or corrected. But even that stage does not necessarily have to be reached. Preventive physiotherapy, such as range of motion exercises, can be very effective on an on-going basis, but *it is not enough*. A therapist can obviously spend a very limited amount of time with each joint on each patient while the contracture producing factors continue to operate the rest of the time.

Rubber-Band Traction Method

The major part of the work must be done by yourself. This, however, does not imply any major hardship or undue effort on your part. You can do a great deal on your own simply by making use of a soft rubber-band or elastic band. The rubber-band traction method can be used as a means of exercising those muscles which you cannot move completely on your own. This technique enables you to move your joints in their full range again and again.

The Shoulder

The range of motion exercises for the shoulder should consist of elevating the arms to full range; for example, ten consecutive times repeated three times daily. This can be done in bed while lying on your back. In this position the force of gravity will enhance the value of the exercise. When necessary, a rubber-band rig (Fig. b)

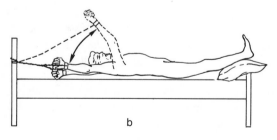

b

or a weight over a pulley is very helpful. When in a wheelchair a rubber-band set up can also be used (Fig. c).

c

The Elbow

Daily exercises in which you fully extend your arm several times a day are easy to perform and are very effective. A rubber-band attached to the bed post is an easy substitute if your elbow extensor muscle is paralyzed (Fig. d). Also, you should avoid prolonged leaning on your flexed elbows to prevent bursitis.

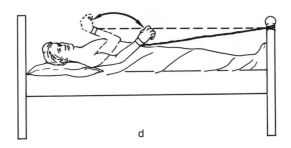

d

The Hand

In the hand, the wrist is the key joint. If you are unable to bring your hand up at the wrist (dorsiflexion), it is necessary to wear a splint. The tendency of the fingers to develop contractures in flexion or extension can be prevented more effectively by proper rubber-band traction than by ranging exercises provided by the therapist. Rubber-bands attached to a glove can provide increased flexor range (Fig. e). They can also be used on special splints to improve extension.

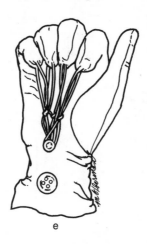

e

However, you must be careful not to manipulate your finger joints too forcefully since this can cause swelling, the formation of abnormal fibrous tissue and eventually decrease your range of motion. Using too strong rubber-band traction can also produce these undesirable effects. You must also be careful of pressure sores at the place where the rubber-band traction is applied. This can be easily prevented by inspecting these areas several times each day. Therefore, the power of the rubber-band must be *weak* but continued for many hours especially at night. If this traction is applied at night, as can be done when you have got some experience, it will leave the hands free for day time activities and still counteract the day long slight pull of the muscles in the opposite direction of the traction. *Power should never be used. Let time with very weak traction do the work.* This simple rubber-band traction technique can both prevent contractures and correct a contracture that has already started to develop providing you have caught it in its early stage.

If you do not use the rubber-band traction method during the night, you should be careful regarding the position of your hand. Above all you should avoid placing your hand under the head in a fist closed position. If your hand is in a fist closed position, you are more likely to develop a contracture, whereas if your hand is flat you can avoid this. If other types of contracture start, let your doctor or therapist know about it as early as possible.

In conclusion, it is hoped that you will find these concepts and recommendations useful in taking proper care of your arms and hands.

12

Possible Developments in the Reconstruction of the Upper Limbs in Tetraplegia

Under normal circumstances this would not have been written until the different procedures suggested had been examined more thoroughly and tested in practise, then being ready for presentation to the patients. The reason for this premature discussion is the age of the author and the limited opportunity he might have to continue the work and the follow-up. He has seen the needs of the patients and in many cases has felt inclined to begin testing out the ideas discussed below. However, progress has to be slow; a further step forward can not be taken until the preceding work has been fully evaluated. It is necessary for the patients to have confidence in the work if advances are to be made, and so progress must be slow. Perhaps a few of the ideas discussed here could be used by others in the future in order to help these so seriously handicapped patients.

The Single Hand Grip

It has already been stated that when using the methods described above only about 60 % of the tetraplegic patients can be surgically helped in some way, but perhaps even more with the new and gratifying experience of the elbow extension. Of the rest, about 15 % were excluded as candidates for surgery due to lack of muscle power for wrist extension. It is possible that the biceps muscle could be used as a wrist extensor, as has already been suggested and performed in different circumstances by Lipscomb et al. 1958 and McDowell (1971). These authors only succeeded in producing weak function and the technique needs to be improved with a better pulley mechanism at the level of the elbow. Certainly an elbow extension is also needed in these cases. (Compare brachioradialis!) Greater than this technical problem, however, is the consideration that supination is of paramount importance to the tetraplegic patient and it must work well. So much depends on his ability to handle objects on a flat supinated hand, even if wrist flexors are lacking. It is probable that in a number of cases a useful supinator muscle is present where brachioradialis is less than grade 4. Supinator alone could be tested if the action of the biceps as the stronger supinator was temporarily blocked by local anesthetic. Alternatively, the coracobrachialis muscle, which is frequently present, could be used as a supinator, elongated with a free tendon graft to the old biceps insertion, thus substituting for the biceps. The brachialis muscle alone is quite strong enough as an elbow flexor, but it does not have adequate amplitude to function as a wrist extensor motor in a surgical procedure. Clearly the biceps, if used as a wrist extensor, must be able to perform this function even when the elbow is flexed at least 90 degrees.

Another consideration is that I may have been too cautious about the use of muscle transfer and flexor tenodesis to the four ulnar fingers. I have certainly seen cases where patients have been satisfied with the result of this surgery, but there have also been others where it led to unwanted results, to finger contracture and also with transfer from bed to wheelchair. Maybe a careful amalgamation between the other methods described in the chapter on bibliography and the method described in this book could offer additional help to some patients. Obviously, this is a field only for surgeons with major experience in surgery in tetraplegia.

The mobilization of the gliding surfaces around tendons which have been involved in surgical procedures of different kinds is always a problem in hand surgery. It is still more so in the surgery of tetraplegia as the patient must do this mobilization with his own, very weak muscles. It is possible that surgical help could be extended to cases with less power available if the postoperative mobilization could be therapeutically assisted. A possibility which does not seem to have been tried yet is the electrical muscle stimulation performed by the patient himself with appliances similar to those used for peroneal insufficiency. This stimulation could also be applied directly to the muscles no longer connected to the central neurone, not to get function, but to help mobilization of adhesions around the active neighbor. In a similar way the muscles to be transferred could certainly be better trained before surgery.

The Two-Hand Grip

Not infrequently, in patients with high lesions who cannot be given a single hand grip by surgical intervention, pectoral and subscapular muscles are too weak to bring both hands together to produce a two-hand grip. It might be possible to produce active adduction of the arms against each other by moving the proximal end of the long head of biceps to the middle of the clavicle. The patient would need to be stabilized in a wheelchair by some other means than hooking his arm behind the handle. Remember the value of the elbow extensor procedure for this group of patients.

The Elbow Extensors

When the whole deltoid is transferred for elbow extension in two operating sessions the total power is much stronger than when only the posterior part is used. No loss of abduction seems to occur following this secondary transfer. It would seem worthwhile, therefore, to try to transfer the whole deltoid to the triceps tendon as a single procedure. A different technique must be developed because no simple suturing of the muscle to the tendon graft would stand up to the pull of the strong deltoid muscle. I have used a new technique in just one case, but it is too early to evaluate the final result yet; therefore, I cannot recommend it on the basis of such limited experience but I will outline the method I used. The same incision and the same grafts were used as in the routine operation described above. The whole deltoid insertion was freed up with a small bone fragment and the suturing of the grafts followed the usual technique. To prevent the strong muscle from pulling the suture apart a stainless steel twisted wire was woven back and forth through the deltoid tendon in such a way that it got a good grip around the bony fragment. It was led distally along the humerus and here it was taken through a borehole and back again and the ends were twisted together. In this way the muscle pull was taken up by the wire and was prevented from pulling the tendon suture apart. The twisted wire ends were brought out through the incision which was sutured in the ordinary way. Treatment in plaster was also unchanged and the plaster was removed six weeks later and the arm was washed. The following day the wire was followed distally through a small incision to the point where the twisting ended. The loop was divided and the whole wire system could then be withdrawn quite easily. The wound was closed and training commenced the next day just as in the routine used earlier.

The "Push-up" Function

The importance of this function can hardly be overestimated in transfers and in preventing pressure sores. It is based much more on muscles able to pull down shoulders than on a triceps function. Not infrequently, a teres major seems to be present and useful in cases where latissimus and the pectoral muscles are insufficient. Perhaps the scapular insertion of the teres major could be shifted to posterior parts of the ribs at an adequate level or by grafts attached to the crista and so assist a push-up. The nerve supply does not seem to speak against such a transfer and the "extra" power needed is often quite limited.

References

Buck-Gramcko, D.: Besserung der Greiffähigkeit der Hand bei den Tetraplegicern. Chir. Plast. et Reconstr., 3: 68, 1967

Curtis, R. M.: Tendon transfers in the patient with spinal cord injury. Orth. Clin. North America 5:415, 1974

DeBenedetti, M.: Restoration of elbow extension in the quadriplegic patient using the Moberg technique. Paper given at the Annual Meeting of the American Society for Surgery of the Hand in Dallas 1978

Dolphin, J. A.: Restoration of thumb-finger pinch in the quadriplegic hand by multiple tenodeses. A report of six cases. J. Bone J. Surg., 52 – A: 1060, 1970 (Abstract)

Freehafer, A. A.: Care of hands in cervical spinal cord injuries. Paraplegia 7: 118, 1969

Freehafer, A. A. and W. A. Mast: Transfer of the brachioradialis to improve wrist extension in high spinal cord injury. J. Bone Jt. Surg., 49-A: 648, 1967

Freehafer, A. A.; E. Von Haam and V. Allen: Tendon transfers to improve grasp in cervical spinal cord injury patients. J. Bone Jt. Surg., 56-A: July 1974

Granit, R.: The functional role of muscle spindles-facts and hypotheses. Brain 98: 531, 1975

Grigg, P., G. A. Finerman and L. H. Riley: Joint position sense after total hip replacement. J. Bone Jt. Surg. 55-A: 1016, 1973

Guttmann, L.: Spinal cord injuries. Blackwell, Oxford 1973

Hanson, R. W. and W. R. Franklin: Sexual loss in relation to other functional losses for spinal cord injured males. Arch. Phys. Med. Rehabil. 57: 291, 1976

Henderson, E. D., P. R. Lipscomb, E. C. Elkins, A. M. Auerbach, J. L. Magness: Review of the results of surgical treatment of patients with tetraplegia. Personal communication and J. Bone Jt. Surg. 52-A: 1059, 1970

House, J. H., F. W. Gwathmey and D. K. Lundsgaard: Restoration of strong grasp and lateral pinch in tetraplegia due to spinal cord injury. J. of Hand Surg. I: 152, 1976

Lamb, D. W.: The management of upper limb in cervical cord injuries. In proceedings of a symposium held in the Royal College of Surgeons of Edinburgh, June 7 and 8, 1963. London, Morrison and Gibbs Ltd 1963

Lamb, D. W. and R. M. Landry: The hand in quadriplegia. The Hand 3: 31, 1971

Lamb, D. W. and R. M. Landry: The hand in quadriplegia. Paraplegia 9: 204, 1972

Lamb, D. W.: Personal communication.

Lipscomb, P. R., E. C. Elkins and E. D. Henderson: Tendon transfers to restore function of hands in tetraplegia, especially after fracture-dislocation of the sixth cervical vertebra on the seventh. J. Bone Jt. Surg. 40-A: 1071, 1958

Maury, M., M. Guillamat and N. François: Our experience of upper limb transfers in cases of tetraplegia. Paraplegia 11: 245, 1973

McDowell, Ch.: Tendon transfer to augment wrist extension in the tetraplegic patient. Proceedings Veterans Administration Spinal Cord Injury Conference. 18: 78, 1971

McDowell, Ch.: Personal Communication.

Michaelis, L. S.: Orthopaedic surgery of the limbs in paraplegia. Springer, Berlin 1964

Moberg, E.: Criticism and study of methods for examining sensibility in the hand. Neurology 12: 8, 1962

Moberg, E.: Dringliche Handchirurgie. Thieme 1968

Moberg, E.: Fingers were made before forks. The Hand 4, 201, 1972

Moberg, E.: Surgical treatment for absent single hand grip and elbow extension in quadriplegia. J. Bone Jt. Surg. 57-A: 196, 1975

Moberg, E.: Reconstructive hand surgery in tetraplegia, stroke and cerebral palsy: Some basic concepts in physiology and neurology. J. of Hand Surg. 1: 29, 1976

Moberg, E.: Editorial. The Hand 9, 3. Oct. 1977

Moberg, E.: Sensibility in reconstructive limb surgery. Mosby, St Louis. 1978 (forthcoming)

Moberg, E.: Where to localize the receptors for proprioception of the human hand? (forthcoming)

Nickel, V. L., J. Perry and A. L. Garrett: Development of useful function in the severely paralyzed hand. J. Bone Jt. Surg. 45-A: 933, 1963

Perry, J.: Surgical treatment of the paralytic Hand. In: The Total Care of Spinal Cord Injuries. ed. by D. S. Pierce and V. H. Nickel. Little, Brown and Co., Boston 1977

Riordan, D.: Surgical reconstruction of secondary deformities of the hand. In: Surgical rehabilitation in leprosy, ed. by. F. McDowell and C. D. Enna. Williams and Wilkins, Boston 1974

Selander, D.: Catheter technique in axillary plexus block. Presentation of a new method. Acta Anaesthesiol. Scand. 21: 324–329, 1977

Street, D. M. and H. D. Stambaugh: Finger flexor tenodesis. Clin. Orthop. 13: 155, 1959

Zancolli, E. A.: Structural and dynamic bases of hand surgery. Lippingcott, Philadelphia, 1968

Zancolli, E. A.: Correccion de la "Garra" digital por paralisis intrinseca. La operation del "Lazo". Acta Ortopedica Latinoamericana I: 65, 1974

Zancolli, E. A.: Surgery for the quadriplegic hand with active, strong wrist extension preserved. A study of 97 cases. Clin. Orthop. 112: 101, 1975

Zancolli, E. A.: Personal communication.

Zrubecky, G.: Operative und konservative Wiederherstellung einer Freifform von schlaff gelähmten Händen bei Halsmarkgeschädigten. Handchirurgie 4: 71, 1972

Zrubecky, G.: Die Hand des Tetraplegikers. Unfallheilkunde 79: 45−54, 1976

Subject Index